KNITTING WITH
The Color Guys

KAFFE FASSETT
BRANDON MABLY

KNITTING WITH
The Color Guys

INSPIRATION, IDEAS, AND PROJECTS
FROM THE KAFFE FASSETT STUDIO

sixth&springbooks
NEW YORK

To all those knitters who enjoy
colorwork as much as we do

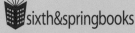
sixth&springbooks
161 Avenue of the Americas New York, NY 10013
sixthandspringbooks.com

EDITORIAL DIRECTOR
Joy Aquilino

DESIGNER
Anne Wilson

MANAGING EDITOR
Wendy Williams

PRINCIPAL
PHOTOGRAPHY
Debbie Patterson

SENIOR EDITOR
Michelle Bredeson

ADDITIONAL
PHOTOGRAPHY
Steven Wooster

ART DIRECTOR
Diane Lamphron

EDITORIAL ASSISTANT
Alexandra Joinnides

VICE PRESIDENT,
PUBLISHER
Trisha Malcolm

PROJECT MANAGER
Susan Berry

CREATIVE DIRECTOR
Joe Vior

PATTERN WRITER/EDITOR
Sarah Hatton

PRODUCTION MANAGER
David Joinnides

TECHNICAL
ILLUSTRATIONS
Jen Arnall-Culliford

PRESIDENT
Art Joinnides

Library of Congress Catalog Control Number:
2011936715

ISBN 978-1-936096-37-4

MANUFACTURED IN CHINA

3 5 7 9 10 8 6 4 2

FIRST EDITION

contents

"full-on color"

Brandon joined my studio in 1991, giving up his career in catering to do so. With only a newborn fascination for design and color, he quickly picked up knitting, needlepoint, rag-rug making, and patchwork. After teaching with me for five years, Brandon took over all the knitting classes and began producing his own books on the craft.

After collaborating for twenty years, we decided the time had come to create a collection together, and this book is the result. It's been very stimulating, knitting ideas together and finding good locations and settings to show them off.

We have done several motifs in two or more colorways to suggest that many varieties of moods can be achieved with these concepts, so you can make our designs work for your personal color taste. A throw or set of cushions should be the highlight of your room. It's a great thrill to make objects that give quality to your everyday life—it's an even bigger charge to make something for someone you love or whose sensibilities you admire or respond to. I always feel that making a rich, colorful object for someone I feel in tune with brings me closer to that person as the work grows under my fingers. It becomes highly motivating work. But then any knitted pattern does the same for both Brandon and me. We can't wait to get to the next motif, the next set of colors—knitting in a monochrome palette is really arduous for us.

Those of you who have never created larger pieces should experience quite an adventurous excitement as your throw or bedcover takes shape. The "killer" rows are the first five to ten before you get enough on your needles to see actual shapes and colors forming. As you progress, especially if choosing your own colors, put the work up on a work board so you can see it from a distance. Remember that the whole thing changes as you add more, so don't judge too harshly till you have at least ten inches of knitting on those needles.

If you have made a really awkward choice of color that disturbs the harmony of your other tones, you can always carefully duplicate stitch (Swiss darn) over that section with a better color, saving you having to pull it apart and start again. We often have false starts where there are several dissonant choices that are too light or dark for our mood. So, we'll just start again and improve. The second attempt goes faster because we have had a rehearsal and are more confident about the color combination.

As I look at Brandon's pieces in this book, I see his graphic confidence in pattern carrying the day. He uses fewer colors and a more contrast-making, bold use of geometry. I feel this might well appeal to knitters who are nervous of my full-on color schemes! His checkerboard ensemble (see page 26) will strike a chord, especially if done in the knitter's own choice of colors. Since Brandon uses fewer tones than I do, it is much easier to switch any of his patterns to another color scheme. His multistripe cushion (see page 62) could be expanded to become a dramatic throw using larger needles, chunky yarn, and a double width for each stripe. The pattern for his dotty cushions (see page 90) could be treated as squares and sewn together to create a spicy, fun bedcover. We both hope you will play with these ideas in any way that occurs to you as you sit down with your own yarn stash.

KAFFE FASSETT

"trying new ideas"

After meeting with Trisha Malcolm, our publisher at SoHo Publishing, Kaffe and I decided to work together on a book to make knitted items that were not garments. The idea excited both Kaffe and me. Before I could turn around, Kaffe had knitted four or five swatches to get a feel for the book samples (a bit daunting for me as I had to attend to the running of the studio, squeezing in design work where I could!). Realizing how important the collaboration could be gave me the motivation to gradually catch up. I was intrigued to see Kaffe using a bright palette in bold contrasts, as opposed to his more usual tone on tone palettes—usually I am the one to reach for the bolder colors and be more graphic with my design work. I particularly like Kaffe's half-circle throw (see page 58), with its hard contrast of jolly colors, making me think of slices of fruit and jaunty fairgrounds.

I can remember a compliment Kaffe gave me, "You dare to be simple," which really charmed me. Somehow I have the confidence to keep trying new ideas. We design directly on the needles from simple charts, but it is very important to pin up the work and stand back to see your progress, rather than judging your work on your lap. As our swatches for this book progressed we would leave them pinned on the studio wall to give us a flavor of how the collection was progressing.

The collection developed organically, which is more fun than an ordered plan, pinning up the work to see if a new idea would become a cushion, throw, or scarf, for example, depending on the weight of the yarn, scale of the pattern, or strength of color, and so on. When the day finally arrived for us to take all the finished pieces out for photography, we could really see how the work looked. For this book, we went down to our friend's house deep in the English countryside and spent two days creating the best settings for our work with our lovely photographer, Debbie Patterson.

We both hope there is something in this book that will tease your imagination and inspire you to pick up the needles and have a go.

BRANDON MABLY

soft tones

This chapter uses the delicate, restrained end of the color palette. Spring blossoms, seashells, even silvered wood and beach pebbles fall into this category. There is always a place for faded, whispering color: all-white shabby chic rooms, white or pale gray outfits, or houses constructed from very natural, weathered wood or stone with succulents in the garden. The following projects include the delicate hues of Brandon's baby blanket on a creamy ivory base; his fingerless gloves in honey and silver tones; followed by his jaunty checkerboard ensemble of hat, leg warmers, and wrist warmers. I contribute to the mélange with a mohair/silk yarn scarf in Easter-egg colors and a sock yarn striped stole in soft pink, baby blues, and cream.

multistripe stole

The idea for this came from 1920s beads made of rolled magazine papers. An elongated triangle of colored paper is rolled up to create a long bead tapered at each end. The colors appear at random, from the colored photographs and print of the magazine pages. The effect of splintered speckles of color is not unlike this stole. This simple-to-knit length of knitting is achieved by alternating two multicolored yarns at a time. There should be a contrast between them, but occasionally the colors will merge, making the knitting process mysterious and fun. You could try this with any sock yarn or space-dyed yarn, or solid colors if you want a really dramatic, sharp effect. I personally love these soft pinks, blues, and creams with odd brown, maroon, and navy depths for dramatic texture. There is sea green and gray running through this that really gives it a soft tone. SEE PAGE 28 FOR PATTERN.

LEFT The fine stripes are softened by using a hand-dyed effect sock yarn to create a romantic stole, set off here by the delicate flowers of the Chinoiserie wallpaper and the elegant pink-flowered teapot.

RIGHT The pastel stripes on the stole sing out on this weathered chair against a bright camellia bush.

triangle baby blanket

This design by Brandon is a new take on the triangle shape I have used in the past, starting with the designs called Super Triangle, where I did triangles in different scales. Here is Brandon on his design: "I fancied the idea of playing with the gorgeous *Summer Tweed* yarns to create a baby blanket or throw. The light colors give me a nice wide-open shape where the simple rows of triangles carry the color in jaunty fashion. The final result reminds me of a yacht regatta with sails of sugared-almond tones. I was delighted to find this flowering magnolia tree to photograph it in. The feathery blossoms make a perfect setting for this creamy concoction."
SEE PAGE 30 FOR PATTERN.

OPPOSITE The shot we took of Brandon's baby blanket in the magnolia tree could not have found a more perfect setting, the delicate flowers echoing its creamy soft tones.
BELOW (LEFT, CENTER, AND RIGHT) The mosaic artist at whose home we photographed it has a wonderful collection of blue-and-white china, which also complements the colors of this blanket beautifully.
OVERLEAF Some of our collection of Chinese porcelain.

zigzag fingerless gloves

Brandon's fingerless gloves pick up on the zigzag design we both love. Here is what Brandon has to say about them: "My twin sister had mentioned to me how much she enjoyed wearing a pair of finely knitted fingerless gloves I'd given her for Christmas. I see zigzags often on my travels, such as the tiled roof of the cathedral in Vienna, which is done in dark and light slates. Since we were using zigzag motifs, I thought I'd do a different slant on it. I wanted to keep the pattern small-scale, so I chose *Cotton Glace* yarn in sunny tones with accents of cool silver and powder blue, adding a single-stitch zigzag for a lacy look. This is ideal to work as a two-color row Fair Isle pattern, in many color schemes."

SEE PAGE 32 FOR PATTERN.

BELOW LEFT The quiet tones of this cottage windowsill act as a foil for the more vibrant colors in the zigzag pattern of the gloves.

BELOW RIGHT This little decoration captures the gold and turquoise flashes of color in the gloves.

RIGHT The shabby-chic, rusty painted chair picks up the colors of the stripes.

mossy stole

Kidsilk Haze is seductive, gossamer, feathery. The very thin fiber is knitted on a needle seemingly too large, but the fiber fills out the stitches, leaving a lacy filament. I chose earthy moss tones for this stole, adding pink and rust. It is warm as toast, though light as a feather to wear. I see it worn with tweeds, plaids, or even as a shawl over a brown or khaki waxed jacket. For those who enjoy a head drape, it would make a wonderful turban or long cowl, one end hanging down, the other thrown over the shoulder to show the repeat stripe to advantage. For people who love to wear color, pair it with purple or deep rust. It could also be a great highlight on a steel-gray outfit. When you're not wearing it, drape it over a large chair back or couch. *Kidsilk Haze* comes in a gorgeous range of colors, so do try it in deep rich jewel tones, or in grays with pearly shimmers of soft pastels.

SEE PAGE 34 FOR PATTERN.

LEFT You don't have to look too hard to see where we found the inspiration for the colors in this stole! The pottery stash in the painting studio at home says it all.

RIGHT The warm, mossy notes in this delicate stole are emphasized by the earthy colors of the chenille sofa.

opal dot scarf

The *Kidsilk* range of yarn by Rowan offers a scintillating array of colors to play with. I've made this scarf on the narrow side, but you could easily make a wider scarf or a stole in the same structure. You could also knit this as a cushion pattern. It's a dead easy way to try your first Fair Isle knitting if you have not gone there before. You can see that these pearly tones go very well on taupe, cream, or silver gray, but the dot pattern also appears in a very dark palette in the last chapter (see page 140), demonstrating how versatile this formula is. Choose a base color that works well with other tones—perhaps maroon, rust, magenta, and crimson tones with black and ochre dots, or cobalt, turquoise, deep green, and navy with maroon and periwinkle dots.

SEE PAGE 37 FOR PATTERN.

OPPOSITE I love the way the misty gray tones in this scarf help to make the brighter shades come alive.
BELOW LEFT When the scarf is worn with a soft blue dress, the pink and lime green really bounce out.
BELOW RIGHT The scarf tones echo the colors in this old blue-and-white jug full of subtle pastel flowers.

checkerboard ensemble

This checkerboard collection epitomizes Brandon's sense of geometry. Here is Brandon's story of his design: "I couldn't resist playing with a checkerboard pattern again. To a lot of people I suppose a checkerboard reminds them of a game board. But broken up with other shades, such as cool gray, robin's-egg blue, and a row of lime moss green, it can give a cool palette a sparkle. It is ideal for using as a border on a garment, or as I have here, as leg and wrist warmers. A snappy hat with a striped crown tops off the ensemble. This is a great project for beginners, as it only has two colors per row to deal with. I'm a big fan of this type of simple pattern. We have used it on garments, fabric design, and patchwork. It is great to play with in different weights of yarn to change the scale of the motif."

SEE PAGES 38, 40 AND 41 FOR PATTERNS.

LEFT The little checks in this design are set off by the striped ribs and the top of the fez-style hat. The flashes of lime and magenta really bring it to life. RIGHT I love the geometry of this marquetry table. It lets you see why Brandon's modern take on an ancient design works so well.

multistripe stole

If you haven't tried my hand-dyed effect sock yarn for Regia yet, then you'll see that you can do a lot more than knit socks with it! It is just perfect for this gently graduated striped stole, as it softens the colors without removing their liveliness.

SKILL LEVEL ◖■■◻◗

FINISHED SIZE
27 x 75"/69 x 190cm

YARN
1 x 3½oz/100g skein (approx. 460yd/420m) each of Regia *Design Line Hand-dye Effect* (75% merino wool; 25% nylon) (**1**) in:
A – Balloon 8851
B – Fog 8853
F – Rock Garden 8850
J – Fuschia 8852
1 x 3½oz/100g skein (approx. 460yd/420m) each of Regia *Design Line* random stripe (70% wool; 25% polyamide; 5% acrylic) (**1**) in:
C – Sizzle 2901
D – Moor 2905
E – Delphinium 2904
G – Anthracite 2903
H – Snappy 2900

NEEDLES
1 pair size 2/3 (3mm) knitting needles
1 size 2/3 (3mm) circular knitting needle

GAUGE
29 sts and 37 rows = 4"/10cm measured over St st using size 2/3 (3mm) needles *or size to obtain correct gauge.*

STOLE
Using A, cast on 194 sts.
Knit 4 rows.
Beg with a K row and working in St st throughout, cont as foll:
Rows 1 and 2 Using B.
Rows 3 and 4 Using C.
Rep last 4 rows twice more.
Rows 13 and 14 Using F.
Rows 15 and 16 Using J.
Rep last 4 rows 4 times more.
Rows 33 and 34 Using C.
Rows 35 and 36 Using J.
Rep these 4 rows 4 times more.
Rows 53 and 54 Using C.
Rows 55 and 56 Using F.
Rep these 4 rows 4 times more.
These rows give you an idea of how to set your stripes. The only rule is to carry 1 color through 2 sets of pattern as set. Cont until work measures 74½"/189cm or length required, ending with RS facing for next row.
Knit 5 rows in A.
Bind off knitwise on WS.

EDGING (both alike)
Using circular needle and A, pick up 612 sts up each side of stole.
Knit 4 rows.
Bind off knitwise on WS.
Press as described on the ball band.

triangle baby blanket

Rowan *Summer Tweed* yarn is just right for this baby blanket, and the chalkiness of the color range plays well into any pastel designs.

SKILL LEVEL ◖■■■▭

FINISHED SIZE
32½ x 39½"/82 x 100cm

YARN
Rowan *Summer Tweed* (70% silk; 30% cotton) 〔4〕
3 x 1¾oz/50g skeins (each approx. 131yd/120m) in:
A – Oats 508
1 x 1¾oz/50g skein (approx. 131yd/120m) each in:
B – Rush 507
C – Swirl 548
D – Raffia 515
E – Powder 500
F – Blueberry 525
G – Sweet Pea 543
H – Butterball 538
I –   Reed 514

NEEDLES AND EXTRAS
1 pair size 8 (5mm) knitting needles
1 size 7 (4.5mm) crochet hook
Piece of backing fabric

GAUGE
16 sts and 23 rows = 4"/10cm measured over St st using size 8 (5mm) needles *or size to obtain correct gauge.*

BLANKET
Using A, cast on 125 sts.
Beg with a K row, working in St st throughout, work in patt as

set on chart from row 1 to 92.
Repeat rows 21 to 92 once, then rows 21 to 56 once more, ending with RS facing for next row.
Now work rows 93 to 112 once, ending with RS facing for next row.
Bind off.

FINISHING
Press as described on the ball band.
Using size 7 (4.5mm) crochet hook and C, work 1 round of single crochet around entire edge of blanket, slip stitch to

first edge to join, work 2 ch and work another round of single crochet around blanket, slip stitch to join, then fasten off. Cut a piece of backing fabric the same size as your blanket. Press a seam the same width as your crochet edge and sew the fabric in position to the back of the blanket just inside the crochet edge.

KEY

☐ Yarn A: Knit on RS, Purl on WS

☒ Yarn B: Knit on RS, Purl on WS

◆ Yarn C: Knit on RS, Purl on WS

❘ Yarn D: Knit on RS, Purl on WS

☐ Yarn E: Knit on RS, Purl on WS

▬ Yarn F: Knit on RS, Purl on WS

✳ Yarn G: Knit on RS, Purl on WS

○ Yarn H: Knit on RS, Purl on WS

▦ Yarn J: Knit on RS, Purl on WS

zigzag fingerless gloves

The relatively fine *Cotton Glace* yarn is great for gloves and has a good color range to choose from, too. The mercerized cotton gives definition to the pattern: soft tones create the background stripes and a sharper contrast defines the zigzags.

SKILL LEVEL ◼◼◻◻◻

FINISHED SIZE
8¼"/21cm circumference, 8½"/22cm deep

YARN
1 x 1¾oz/50g skein (approx. 126yd/115m) each of Rowan *Cotton Glace* (100% cotton) (2) in:
A – Oyster 735
B – Chalk 827
C – Ecru 723
D – Dawn Grey 831
E – Ochre 833
F – Persimmon 832
G – Umber 838
H – Ivy 812
J – Heather 828
K – Dijon 739

NEEDLES
1 pair size 2 (2.75mm) knitting needles
1 pair size 3 (3.25mm) knitting needles
1 set size 3 (3.25mm) double-pointed knitting needles

GAUGE
23 sts and 32 rows = 4"/10cm measured over St st using size 3 (3.25mm) needles *or size to obtain correct gauge.*

RIGHT GLOVE
Using size 2 (2.75mm) needles and A, cast on 49 sts.
Row 1 (RS) K1, * p1, k1, rep from * to end.
Row 2 * P1, k1, rep from * to last st, p1.
These 2 rows set rib.
Work 4 rows more in rib.
Change to B and work 2 rows in rib.
Change to A and work 4 rows in rib.
Change to size 3 (3.25mm) needles, beg with a K row and working in St st throughout, cont as foll:
Work next 40 rows as set on chart, ending with RS facing for next row.
Next row Working in patt as set on chart, work 26 sts, leave the last 12 sts on a holder, patt to end.
Next row Working in patt as set on chart, work 23 sts, cast on 6 sts, patt to end. *43 sts.*
Work rows 43 to 48 as set on chart, ending with RS facing for next row.

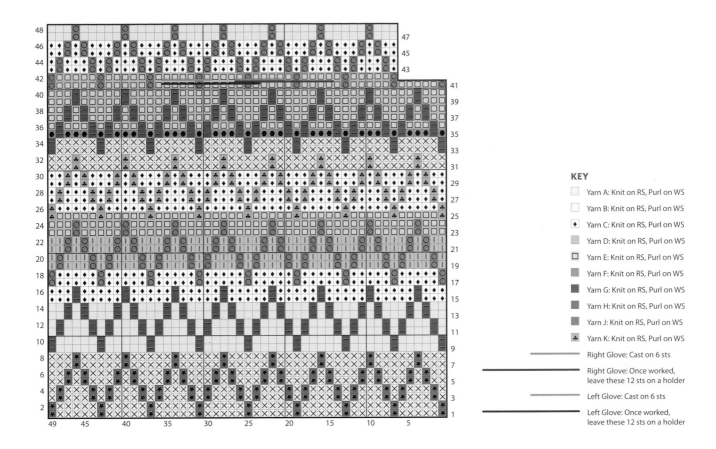

KEY

☐ Yarn A: Knit on RS, Purl on WS

☐ Yarn B: Knit on RS, Purl on WS

◆ Yarn C: Knit on RS, Purl on WS

▨ Yarn D: Knit on RS, Purl on WS

☐ Yarn E: Knit on RS, Purl on WS

▨ Yarn F: Knit on RS, Purl on WS

▪ Yarn G: Knit on RS, Purl on WS

▪ Yarn H: Knit on RS, Purl on WS

▪ Yarn J: Knit on RS, Purl on WS

♣ Yarn K: Knit on RS, Purl on WS

——— Right Glove: Cast on 6 sts

——— Right Glove: Once worked, leave these 12 sts on a holder

——— Left Glove: Cast on 6 sts

——— Left Glove: Once worked, leave these 12 sts on a holder

Change to size 2 (2.75mm) needles and work 6 rows in rib.
Bind off in rib.

Using size 3 (3.25mm) double-pointed needles and E, pick up and knit 4 sts from 6 sts cast on above thumb, now work across these 4 sts along with 12 sts on a holder as set:

Round 1 *K1, p1, rep from * to end.

Work 5 rounds more in rib.

Bind off in rib.

LEFT GLOVE

Using size 2 (2.75mm) needles and A, cast on 49 sts.

Row 1 (RS) K1, * p1, k1, rep from * to end.

Row 2 * P1, k1, rep from * to last st, p1.

These 2 rows set rib.

Work 4 rows more in rib.

Change to B and work 2 rows in rib.

Change to A and work 4 rows in rib.

Change to size 3 (3.25mm) needles, beg with a K row and

working in St st throughout cont as foll:

Work next 40 rows as set on chart, ending with RS facing for next row.

Next row Working in patt as set on chart, work 35 sts, leave the last 12 sts on a holder, patt to end.

Next row Working in patt as set on chart, work 14 sts, cast on 6 sts, patt to end. *43 sts.*

Work rows 43 to 48 as set on chart, ending with RS facing for next row.

Change to size 2 (2.75mm) needles and work 6 rows in rib.
Bind off in rib.

Using size 3 (3.25mm) double-pointed needles and E, pick up and knit 4 sts from 6 sts cast on above thumb, now work across these 4 sts along with 12 sts on a holder as set:

Round 1 *K1, p1, rep from * to end.

Work 5 rounds more in rib.

Bind off in rib.

Press as described on the ball band.

mossy stole

The range of colors in this yarn really makes it easy to create delicate yet vibrant stripes, as the nature of the yarn helps to blend the colors. You could make a shorter, narrower version working your own preferred colors.

SKILL LEVEL ◧■□□

FINISHED SIZE

20 x 106¼"/51 x 270cm

YARN

1 x 1¾oz/50g skein (approx. 229yd/210m) each of Rowan *Kidsilk Haze* (70% super kid mohair; 30% silk) 🔘 in:

A – Elegance 577
B – Jelly 597
C – Mist 636
D – Marmalade 596
E – Blood 627
F – Majestic 589
G – Anthracite 639
H – Flower 643
J – Meadow 581
K – Ember 644
L – Garden 645

NEEDLES

1 pair size 6 (4mm) knitting needles

GAUGE

20 sts and 31 rows = 4"/10cm measured over St st using size 6 (4mm) needles *or size to obtain correct gauge.*

STOLE

Using A, cast on 102 sts. Beg with a K row, working in St st throughout, work in patt as set on chart, work rows 1 to 218 once, then rows 9 to 218 twice more, or until scarf reaches desired length, ending with RS facing for next row. Bind off.

KEY

■ Yarn A: Knit on RS, Purl on WS
■ Yarn B: Knit on RS, Purl on WS
□ Yarn C: Knit on RS, Purl on WS
▨ Yarn D: Knit on RS, Purl on WS
■ Yarn E: Knit on RS, Purl on WS
■ Yarn F: Knit on RS, Purl on WS
■ Yarn G: Knit on RS, Purl on WS
▣ Yarn H: Knit on RS, Purl on WS
□ Yarn J: Knit on RS, Purl on WS
□ Yarn K: Knit on RS, Purl on WS
□ Yarn L: Knit on RS, Purl on WS
□ Pattern repeat

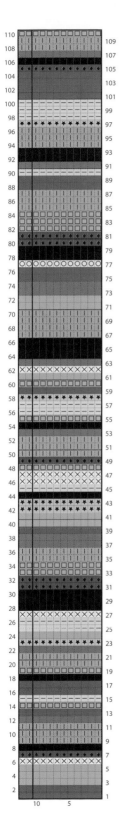

CHART CONTINUED

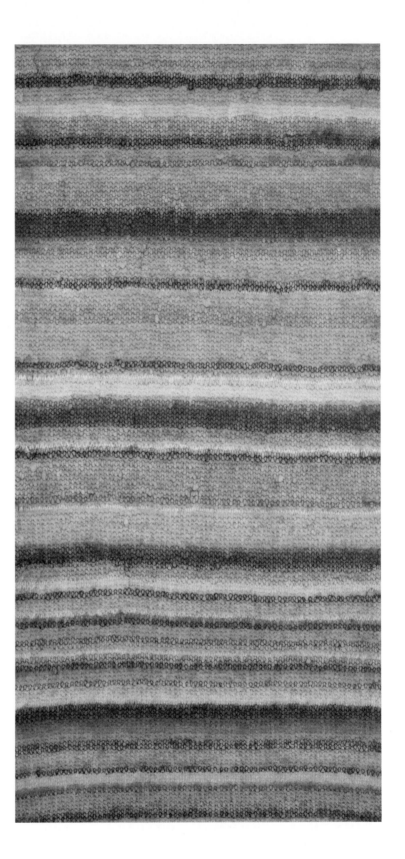

opal dot scarf

This is knitted mostly in *Kidsilk Aura*, the bigger sister of *Kidsilk Haze*, with a few colors in *Kidsilk Haze* held double. If you wish, you could use *Kidsilk Haze* double throughout.

SKILL LEVEL ◼◼◻◻

FINISHED SIZE
11½ x 67"/29 x 170cm

YARN
Rowan *Kidsilk Aura* (75% kid mohair; 25% silk) ④
1 x ¾oz/25g skein (approx. 82yd/75m) each in:
B – Ivory 750
C – Mallard 769
D – Powder 753
E – Vintage 757
F – Coral 774
G – Wheat 752
H – Cypress 755
M – Orchard 771
2 x ¾oz/25g skeins (approx. 82yd/75m) each in:
A – Pumice 768
1 x ¾oz/25g skein (approx. 229yd/210m) of Rowan *Kidsilk Haze* (70% super kid mohair; 30% silk) ③ each in:
J – Garden 645 USED DOUBLE THROUGHOUT
K – Glacier 640 USED DOUBLE THROUGHOUT
See alternative colorway on page 140.

NEEDLES
1 pair size 10½ (7mm) knitting needles

GAUGE
14 sts and 18 rows = 4"/10cm measured over St st on size 10½ (7mm) needles *or size to obtain correct gauge.*

SCARF
Using A, cast on 40 sts.
Knit 2 rows.
Beg with a K row and working in St st throughout, cont as foll:
Rows 1 to 4 Using A.
Row 5 * K2B, k2C, rep from * to end.
Rows 6 to 9 Using D.
Row 10 *P2C, p2B, rep from * to end.
Rows 11 to 14 Using A.
Row 15 As row 5.
Rows 16 to 19 Using E.
Row 20 As row 10.
Rows 21 to 24 Using A.
Row 25 As row 5.
Rows 26 to 29 Using F.
Row 30 As row 10.
Rows 31 to 34 Using A.
Row 35 As row 5.
Rows 36 to 39 Using G.
Row 40 As row 10.
Rows 41 to 44 Using A.
Row 45 As row 5.
Rows 46 to 49 Using H.
Row 50 As row 10.
Rows 51 to 54 Using A.
Row 55 As row 5.
Rows 56 to 59 Using J.
Row 60 As row 10.
Rows 61 to 64 Using A.
Row 65 As row 5.
Rows 66 to 69 Using K.
Row 70 As row 10.
These 70 rows set patt.
Cont in patt as set until work measures approx. 67"/170cm, ending with 4 rows of A and RS facing for next row.
Knit 3 rows.
Bind off knitwise on WS.

checkerboard ensemble

This comprises a hat, leg warmers and wrist warmers. They are knitted using the Fair Isle technique, the thickness of which helps to give the hat its fez-like structure. You could use scraps of your own color choices for the small flashes of color introduced into the pattern. The neat leg warmers are quite fitted, as this shows up the pattern best, but you could always add multiples of 10 stitches to make them wider. If you are new to Fair Isle knitting (see page 170), the fingerless gloves are ideal as you have only the thumb gusset to deal with.

checkerboard hat

SKILL LEVEL ⬤⬤⬤⬜⬜

FINISHED SIZE
To fit average-sized head

YARN
1 x 1¾oz/50g skein (approx. 175yd/160m) each of Rowan *Pure Wool 4 ply* (100% superwash wool) (**1**) in:
A – Black 404
B – Eau di Nil 450
C – Port 437
D – Avocado 419
E – Indigo 410
F – Clay 401

NEEDLES
1 pair size 3 (3.25mm) knitting needles

GAUGE
28 sts and 36 rows = 4"/10cm measured over St st using size 3 (3.25mm) needles *or size to obtain correct gauge.*

PATTERN NOTE
Work using the Fair Isle technique (see page 170).

CHART A

CHART B

KEY

■ Yarn A: Knit on RS, Purl on WS

✕ Yarn B: Knit on RS, Purl on WS

▨ Yarn C: Knit on RS, Purl on WS

Ⅰ Yarn D: Knit on RS, Purl on WS

▦ Yarn E: Knit on RS, Purl on WS

● Yarn F: Knit on RS, Purl on WS

☐ Pattern repeat

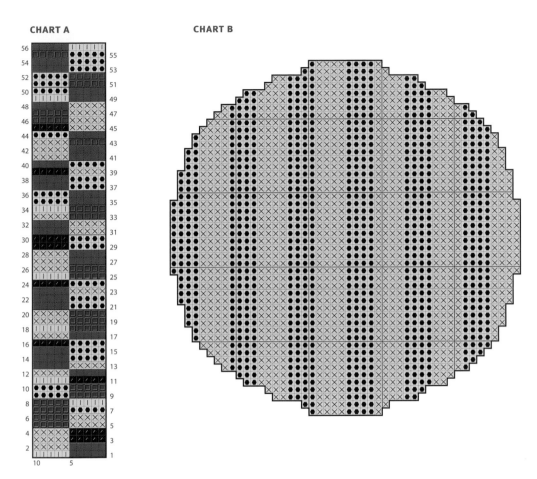

BRIM

Using A, cast on 130 sts.

Row 1 (RS) P2A, * k2B, p2A, rep from * to end.

Row 2 * K2A, p2B, rep from * to last 2 sts, k2A.

These 2 rows set rib.

Work 8 rows more in rib.

Using A, knit 2 rows (to form fold line).

Beg with a K row and working in St st throughout, cont as foll:

Row 1 Working from right to left, work 10 sts as set on row 1 of chart A 13 times.

Row 2 Working from left to right, work 10 sts as set on row 2 of chart A 13 times.

These 2 rows set chart position.

Cont in patt as set on chart until row 36 has been completed, ending with RS facing for next row.

Bind off.

TOP

Using A, cast on 10 sts.

Beg with a K row and working in St st throughout, cont as foll:

Using the Fair Isle technique and working shaping as shown, cont from chart B until row 48 has been completed, ending with RS facing for next row.

Using A, bind off.

FINISHING

Press as described on the ball band.

Join back seam of brim. Sew hat top in position to bound-off edge of brim, easing in position at the same time.

Fold back rib of brim to WS and slip stitch loosely in position.

checkerboard leg warmers

SKILL LEVEL ■■□□

FINISHED SIZE
10 x 14½"/25 x 37cm

YARN
1 x 1¾oz/50g skein (approx. 175yd/160m) each of Rowan *Pure Wool 4 ply* (100% superwash wool) **1** in:

A – Black 404
B – Eau di Nil 450
C – Port 437
D – Avocado 419
E – Indigo 410
F – Clay 401

NEEDLES
1 pair size 3 (3.25mm) knitting needles

GAUGE
28 sts and 36 rows = 4"/10cm measured over St st using size 3 (3.25mm) needles *or size to obtain correct gauge.*

PATTERN NOTE
Work using the Fair Isle technique (see page 170).

LEG WARMERS (make 2)
Using A, cast on 70 sts.
Row 1 (RS) * P2A, k2B, rep from * to last 2 sts, p2A.
Row 2 K2A, * p2B, p2A, rep from * to end.
These 2 rows set rib.
Work 4 rows more in rib.
Beg with a K row and working in St st throughout, cont as foll:
Row 1 Working from right to left, work 10 sts as set on row 1 of chart A 7 times.
Row 2 Working from left to right, work 10 sts as set on row 2 of chart A 7 times.
These 2 rows set chart position.
Cont in patt as set on chart, working 60 row repeat throughout until work measures 13¾"/35cm, ending with RS facing for next row.
Work 8 rows in rib as set.
Using A, bind off.

FINISHING
Press as described on the ball band.
Join back seam.

checkerboard wrist warmers

SKILL LEVEL ◖■■■■▶

FINISHED SIZE
7 x 8"/18 x 20cm

YARN
1 x 1¾oz/50g skein (approx. 175yd/160m) each of Rowan
Pure Wool 4 ply (100% superwash wool) 🔢 in:

A – Black 404
B – Eau di Nil 450
C – Port 437
D – Avocado 419
E – Indigo 410
F – Clay 401

NEEDLES
1 pair size 3 (3.25mm) knitting needles
1 set size 3 (3.25mm) double-pointed knitting needles

GAUGE
28 sts and 36 rows = 4"/10cm measured over St st using
size 3 (3.25mm) needles *or size to obtain correct gauge.*

PATTERN NOTE
Work using the Fair Isle technique (see page 170).

WRIST WARMERS (make 2)
Using size 3 (3.25mm) needles and A, cast on 50 sts.
Row 1 (RS) * P2A, k2B, rep from * to last 2 sts, p2A.
Row 2 K2A, * p2B, k2A, rep from * to end.
These 2 rows set rib.
Work 4 rows more in rib.
Beg with a K row and working in St st throughout, cont as foll:
Row 1 Working from right to left, work 10 sts as set on row 1
of chart A 5 times.
Row 2 Working from left to right, work 10 sts as set on row 2
of chart A 5 times.
These 2 rows set chart position.
Cont in patt as set on chart, work 42 rows more, ending with
RS facing for next row.

Next row Patt as set on chart row 45 for 15 sts (left wrist
warmer) or 25 sts (right wrist warmer), bind off 10 sts, patt to
end.
Next row Patt as set on chart row 46 for 25 sts (left wrist
warmer) or 15 sts (left wrist warmer), cast on 10 sts, patt to
end.
Work rows 47 to 56 as set on chart, ending with RS facing for
next row.
Work 6 rows in rib as set.
Using A, bind off.
Thumbs
Using double-pointed needles and A, pick up and knit 20 sts
evenly all round thumb opening.
Working in rounds not rows, cont as foll:
Round 1 * P2B, k2A, rep from * to end.
Work 5 rounds more in rib.
Using A, bind off.

FINISHING
Press as described on the ball band.
Join side seam.

singing color

These are the wide-awake, exciting colors of childhood. Circuses and carnivals revel in their palette. Floral displays in summer parks and fruit and vegetable markets bring us a joyous abundance of color from the natural world. When it comes to cheering up a room or celebrating a birthday, these colors come into their own. Balloons and candy are often found in these shades. I took the layout for the shadowbox cushion and throw from an antique piece of needlepoint. Its three-dimensional look is created by two tones of the same high colors. The triangle cushion has a sharp geometric look that could grace a carousel or a painted wagon. The half-circle throw is a deliciously graphic conglomeration of split circles in the hues of bright crayons. It's almost African or Indian in mood. The same pattern is so different in dark, smoldering tones in the last chapter (see page 150).

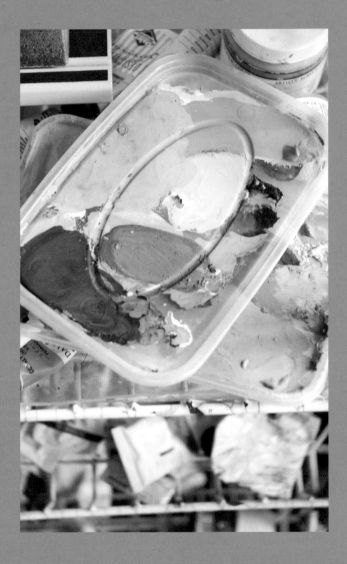

zigzag throw

I often recall the first time Brandon and I visited South Africa. A startlingly handsome lady with a shaved head greeted us at the airport. Around her shoulders was a blanket of wide bands of contrasting colors—hot yellow, deep red, white, black, and cobalt blue. Her wrists, ankles, and neck were adorned with beaded rings in the same colors. She was from the Ndebele tribe, famous for high-contrast blocks of color in their dress and painted on their houses. Nothing fussy, just bold, bold, bold. These large-scale patterns were ideal to use as big yarn pieces—a bold zigzag in this chunky yarn made for a deliciously quick knit designed by Brandon. I don't back or line my knitting, as any knitted work has a life of its own, and if your ends are neatly tucked in, the back texture can be quite attractive on Fair Isle or intarsia work.

SEE PAGE 64 FOR PATTERN.

RIGHT AND OVERLEAF Big and bold zigzag stripes in contrasting colors are the hallmarks of this design by Brandon. The striped borders and a voluptuous multicolored tassel at each corner add the perfect finishing detail. OPPOSITE The simple, strong blocks of color echo the impact of the big zigzags.

shadowbox cushion

Inspired by a scrap of ancient needlepoint I found in a flea market, I have made this design in many different mediums, such as knitting, needlepoint, and patchwork. The piece I bought was in old faded fresco tones of moss, taupe, dull lavender, dusty pinks, and slate blue.

I loved charging up the palette of these high-singing colors with black punctuations. You can see that any colors could work, from all shades of ivory to the other extreme, using darkest navy, wine, peat browns, and bottle greens. You just need a dark and lighter shade of each color to create your shadowbox, and a border color. I think you'll find this as fun to knit as I did. I couldn't wait to enlarge it into the throw on page 50.

At this scale this pattern would make a great vest knitted in country tweed colors, or even black, white, and grays for a jazzy look.

SEE PAGE 66 FOR PATTERN.

LEFT AND RIGHT We found just the right setting for the shadowbox cushion against the mosaic doors of a washstand cabinet (right) with dark and light tones, and on an old chenille design on a sofa (left).

shadowbox throw

Here, I use the same sort of palette in a heavier yarn than the shadowbox cushion on page 48. This could be exciting enlarged further to an afghan or blanket size in even thicker yarns. As I've stated for the shadowbox cushion, you can use any sets of harmonious colors in light and dark to create this exciting geometric design.

When I used the pattern for a quilt in my recent book *Quilts in Sweden*, I employed warm marquetry browns and golds that would also make good knitted blanket colors. Or why not try all stone colors, rather like the pebble mosaics you find in Roman villas? Think of warm pinky grays, blue grays, and green grays with a charcoal for dark areas. Send me a picture if you try it!

SEE PAGE 68 FOR PATTERN.

LEFT The juxtaposition of rich colors against the Arts and Crafts fireplace and wallpaper make just the right setting for the shadowbox throw.
RIGHT Gorgeous old roses and sweet peas against the rich tones of English Moorcroft pottery—an inspiring color mix.

pineapple blanket

In the 1970s I bought a bold kilim rug that featured this pineapple pattern. I used the layout to knit large coats and small-scale sleeveless sweaters. To achieve a more complex coloring, I knitted stripes of merging colors—sometimes I would use up to fifty colors in a coat—quite a challenge!

When I was asked by Rowan to design a special yarn with color changes in long sequences, I was delighted. Fed into this pineapple motif, it totally comes into its own. Using several different color palettes, you sit back amazed at the colors that come up against each other: suddenly a brilliant orange appears next to soft lavender that morphs into a dark green. The trick is to pick hanks of yarn that are harmonious but slightly contrast with each other for the most part. There will be places where the design merges, because colors are close at that point, but the difference soon reappears. You will have leftover colors that can be applied to the next row of pineapples, and if you run out of any hank before completing a motif, look for a leftover similar to the shade where you left off so the join is smoother.

Here is an easy solution to the many complex color changes that I used in those original designs several decades ago.

SEE PAGE 70 FOR PATTERN.

OPPOSITE AND BELOW Don't you just love the way the colors sing out in this pineapple blanket? It is an absolute feast of color and is guaranteed to catch the eye in almost any setting.

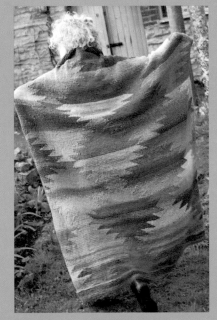

zigzag cushion

The zigzag is one of my favorite geometric patterns to use in knitting, rugs, needlepoint, or patchwork. The Missoni family, the world's most glamorous knitters, have used this motif with great style in their exciting garments. The pattern dances across any surface in its joyous staccato mood. I find the soft contrast I've used here is quietly dramatic. It is a small cushion that can be a highlight on a bed or couch but could easily be expanded into a larger version by using thicker yarn. This pattern would also make a stylish shawl or leg warmers. Think of the color moods you could create with this layout: dark jewels or hot spicy reds; oranges and pinks with emerald and turquoise; or very bold with black and ochre.

SEE PAGE 74 FOR PATTERN.

LEFT The zigzag cushion is set off by the bright Bargello tapestry of the chair and the gloriously overblown flowers of the old Sanderson wallpaper in our London house.
RIGHT Our zigzag cushion echoes the spidery details on this fine Japanese floral cup and saucer.

triangle cushion

This pattern of slightly elongated triangles in sharp colors comes from the world of circuses and folk decoration. When I was in Afghanistan in the 1970s, I stumbled into a courtyard where four men with little buckets of paint were decorating a wagon by painting scenes and flowers surrounded by geometric borders. Each man had a different color and one would circle the wagon painting all the yellow bits followed by a fellow painting the red areas. Then the blue paint was applied by a third man, and so on. It was a rhythmic dance of color, each confident in his task and happy with the exciting results as the rough country wagon was transformed into a magic caravan.

I've loved bright geometric motifs ever since. The sharp contrasts here catch the eye and give us another dancing surface for our rooms, or could be worn as legwarmers, looking like beaded legs of African dancers.

SEE PAGE 76 FOR PATTERN.

RIGHT Bold geometric patterns like those on this woven throw can be found in folk art textiles from many countries. OPPOSITE The cushion has a jewel-like quality in this setting. Note how the triangles pick up the background yellow.

half-circle throw

I decided to do this knit with more contrast than I usually go for. The shape is graphic and a bit cheeky, like slices of oranges and lemons. So I started playing with rather primitive African strong pastels and dark contrasting tones. The colors in *Handknit Cotton* were just the right level of brightness to answer my needs. The yarn is thick enough to make fairly quick progress on this exciting large project. I for one am never happier than when I've got work on the go like this that I can really get my teeth into. I take it with me on my travels and can't wait to see what effect the next sequence of color will add to the emerging design.

SEE PAGE 78 FOR PATTERN.

LEFT AND BELOW LEFT The bright, rounded shapes of the half-circle throw echo the satisfying colors and outlines of simple pottery shapes. BELOW RIGHT The same color palette can be found in our painting studio.

broken stripe scarf

In our design studio, we have several bookshelves stacked high with multicolored books. In front of the books are jars and mugs holding colored marker pens in different sizes along with knitting needles waiting to be used. Right there before us was an idea for a knit using a series of contrasting colors in broken stripes! Brandon's design uses a DK weight yarn, keeping the widths of the stripes the same throughout—the focus is on the color play. He wanted the design to fall off the edge, so added only a couple of rows of crochet for the border. Think of all the color moods you could apply to this vigorous layout.

SEE PAGE 80 FOR PATTERN.

OPPOSITE AND BELOW LEFT Brandon's jazzy broken stripe scarf really stands out against a country willow fence. BELOW RIGHT This close-up detail of the scarf shows off the wonderful, irregular splashes of color.

multistripe cushion

Some years ago we had the fortune to travel to Guatemala, where we found an array of bright and colorful textiles. One of the pieces we returned home with was a cloth bag made up of contrasting stripes in shades of red, bright blue, cream, and yellow. I thought this idea would translate well into a timeless cushion. One way you could make it is to knit striped triangles following the same color sequence and sew them together, arriving at this multiframe design, or knit it in one piece. For this sample, I used a 4-ply *Cotton Glace* in rich colors for a sharp, glassy contrast in the stripes.

SEE PAGE 82 FOR PATTERN.

LEFT This mesmerizing approach to stripes in the multistripe cushion would make a great highlight for any living room.

RIGHT Even the humblest setting can produce inspiring colors, as you can see with this turquoise mosaic backsplash, pink dishwashing basin, and bright flowers.

zigzag throw

Knitted in a really big yarn like Rowan *Big Wool*, this African-inspired throw, with its strongly contrasting colored zigzags, is surprisingly quick to knit.

FINISHED SIZE
68 x 28¾"/173 x 73cm

YARN
6 x 3½oz/100g skeins (each approx. 87yd/80m) each of Rowan *Big Wool* (100% merino wool) **6** in:
A – Zing 037
B – Lipstick 063
C – Vert 054
D – Wild Berry 025
E – Glamour 036

NEEDLES
1 size 15 (10mm) circular knitting needle

GAUGE
8 sts and 12 rows = 4"/10cm measured over St st using size 15 (10mm) circular needle *or size to obtain correct gauge.*

PATTERN NOTE
Work using the intarsia technique (see pages 170 and 172).

THROW
Using A and size 15 (10mm) circular needle, cast on 136 sts. Working back and forth, cont as foll:
Knit 2 rows.
Using B, knit 4 rows AND AT SAME TIME dec 1 st at each end of 1st and 3rd row. *132 sts.*
Using C, knit 4 rows AND AT SAME TIME dec 1 st at each end of 1st and 3rd row. *128 sts.*
Using D, knit 4 rows AND AT SAME TIME dec 1 st at each end of 1st and 3rd row. *124 sts.*
Using E, knit 4 rows AND AT SAME TIME dec 1 st at each end of 1st and 3rd row. *120 sts.*
Beg and ending rows as shown, using the intarsia technique,

working in garter st work 1st 4 rows as set on chart.

Beg with a K row and working in St st throughout cont in patt as set on chart, working the 24-row rep twice, then rows 1 to 22 again, ending with RS facing for next row.

Working in garter st, work 4 rows more in patt, ending with RS facing for next row.

Using E, knit 4 rows AND AT SAME TIME inc 1 st at each end of 1st and 3rd row. *124 sts.*

Using D, knit 4 rows AND AT SAME TIME inc 1 st at each end of 1st and 3rd row. *128 sts.*

Using C, knit 4 rows AND AT SAME TIME inc 1 st at each end of 1st and 3rd row. *132 sts.*

Using B, knit 4 rows AND AT SAME TIME inc 1 st at each end of 1st and 3rd row. *136 sts.*

Using A, knit 3 rows, ending with WS facing for next row.

Bind off knitwise on WS.

SIDE EDGINGS (both alike)

Using E, pick up and knit 58 sts evenly along side edge.

Knit 1 row.

Work 2 rows AND AT SAME TIME inc 1 st at each end of 1st row. *60 sts.*

Using D, knit 4 rows AND AT SAME TIME inc 1 st at each end of 1st and 3rd row. *64 sts.*

Using C, knit 4 rows AND AT SAME TIME inc 1 st at each end of 1st and 3rd row. *68 sts.*

Using B, knit 4 rows AND AT SAME TIME inc 1 st at each end of 1st and 3rd row. *72 sts.*

Using A, knit 3 rows AND AT SAME TIME inc 1 st at each end of 1st and 3rd row, ending with WS facing for next row.

76 sts.

Bind off knitwise on WS.

FINISHING

Press as described on the ball band.

Join seams at each edge of garter st edgings.

Make 4 tassels using a mixture of colors and attach 1 tassel to each corner of throw.

KEY

☐ Knit on RS, Purl on WS, using color as shown

● Purl on RS, Knit on WS, using color as shown

☐ Yarn A

■ Yarn B

☐ Yarn C

■ Yarn D

☐ Yarn E

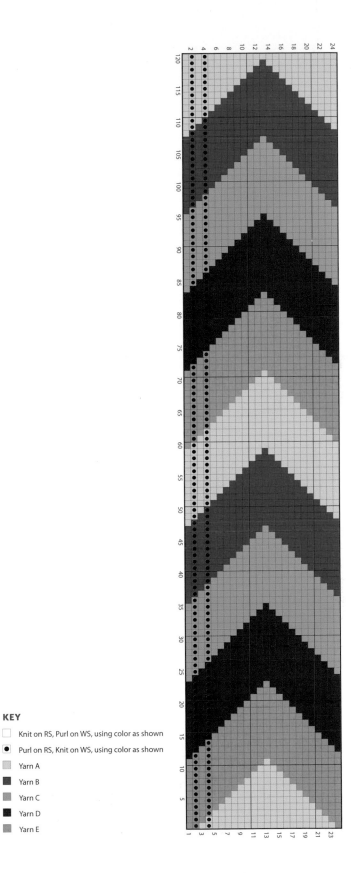

shadowbox cushion

The key to the impact of this cushion lies in the way the series of blocks are placed in diagonal rows. Knitting it in a mercerized cotton like Rowan *Cotton Glace* gives the colors a sharper edge.

SKILL LEVEL ◼◼◼▢

FINISHED SIZE
19¼ x 19"/49 x 48cm

YARN
1 x 1¾oz/50g skein (approx. 126yd/115m) each of Rowan *Cotton Glace* (100% cotton) (❷) in:

A – Dijon 739
B – Nightshade 746
C – Umber 838
D – Dawn Grey 831
E – Bubbles 724
F – Candy Floss 747
G – Ivy 812
H – Shoot 814
J – Baked Red 837
K – Persimmon 832
L – Sky 749
M – Chalk 827

NEEDLES AND EXTRAS
1 pair size 3 (3.25mm) knitting needles
1 piece of fabric, size to match cushion plus ¾"/2cm seam allowance on all sides
Cushion form or stuffing

GAUGE
23 sts and 32 rows = 4"/10cm measured over St st using size 3 (3.25mm) needles *or size to obtain correct gauge.*

CUSHION
Using A and size 3 (3.25mm) needles, cast on 112 sts. Beg with a K row, working in St st throughout, beg and ending rows as shown and working first 22 sts 5 times, then sts 23 and 24 once. Working 25 row rep throughout in colorways as shown on diagram, cont as set until all the squares shown on the color diagram have been worked. Work 2 rows in A.
Bind off.

FINISHING
Press as described on the ball band.
Press seams. With RS facing, sew together the fabric back and knitted front with cushion form or stuffing inside.

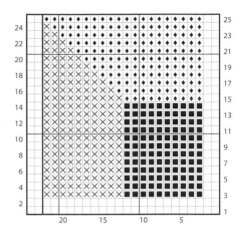

KEY

☐ Color 1: Knit on RS, Purl on WS

■ Color 2: Knit on RS, Purl on WS

☒ Color 3: Knit on RS, Purl on WS

◆ Color 4: Knit on RS, Purl on WS

SQUARE LAYOUT DIAGRAM

5	4	3	2	1
1	5	4	3	2
2	1	5	4	3
3	2	1	5	4
4	3	2	1	5
5	4	3	2	1

Square 1

1 = Yarn A

2 = Yarn B

3 = Yarn C

4 = Yarn D

Square 2

1 = Yarn A

2 = Yarn B

3 = Yarn F

4 = Yarn F

Square 3

1 = Yarn A

2 = Yarn B

3 = Yarn G

4 = Yarn H

Square 4

1 = Yarn A

2 = Yarn B

3 = Yarn J

4 = Yarn K

Square 5

1 = Yarn A

2 = Yarn B

3 = Yarn L

4 = Yarn M

shadowbox throw

The darkest shades in each square create the shadowbox effect. I love the multicolored pattern, but you could also create a more monochrome version—perhaps using earthier colors—if you prefer.

SKILL LEVEL ■■■◻

FINISHED SIZE
29½ x 35"/75 x 89cm

YARN
Rowan *Handknit Cotton* (100% cotton) 〔4〕
6 x 1¾oz/50g skeins (each approx. 93yd/85m) each in:
A – Tope 253
3 x 1¾oz/50g skeins (each approx. 93yd/85m) each in:
B – Turkish Plum 277
1 x 1¾oz/50g skein (approx. 93yd/85m) each in:
C – Slick 313
D – Sugar 303
E – Delphinium 334
F – Raffia 330
G – Gooseberry 219
H – Celery 309
J – Rosso 215
K – Burnt 343
L – Thunder 335
M – Ice Water 239
N – Tangerine Dream 337
P – Linen 205

NEEDLES
1 pair size 6 (4mm) knitting needles
1 size E-4 (3.5mm) crochet hook

GAUGE
20 sts and 28 rows = 4"/10cm measured over St st using size 6 (4mm) needles *or size to obtain correct gauge.*

THROW
Using A, cast on 134 sts.
Beg with a K row, working in St st throughout, beg and ending rows as shown and working first 22 sts 6 times, then sts 23 and 24 once, cont as foll:
Working the 25-row rep throughout in colorways as shown on diagram, cont as set until all the squares shown on the color diagram have been worked.
Work 2 rows in A.
Bind off.

EDGING
Using size E-4 (3.5mm) crochet hook and A, work 1 round of single crochet around entire edge of throw, slip stitch to first stitch to join.
Next round Work 2 ch, then work 1 round of single crochet around entire edge of throw, slip stitch to first stitch to join.
Rep this round twice, then work 4 rounds in B.
Fasten off.
Press as described on the ball band.

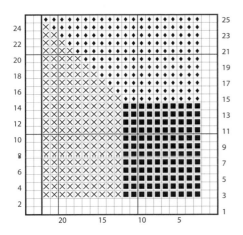

25 ... **23** ... **21** ... **19** ... **17** ... **15** ... **13** ... **11** ... **9** ... **7** ... **5** ... **3** ... **1**

24 22 20 18 16 14 12 10 8 6 4 2

20 15 10 5

KEY

☐ Color 1: Knit on RS, Purl on WS
■ Color 2: Knit on RS, Purl on WS
☒ Color 3: Knit on RS, Purl on WS
◆ Color 4: Knit on RS, Purl on WS

SQUARE LAYOUT DIAGRAM

4	3	2	1	6	5
5	4	3	2	1	6
6	5	4	3	2	1
1	6	5	4	3	2
2	1	6	5	4	3
3	2	1	6	5	4
4	3	2	1	6	5
5	4	3	2	1	6
6	5	4	3	2	1

Square 1
1 = Yarn A
2 = Yarn B
3 = Yarn C
4 = Yarn D

Square 2
1 = Yarn A
2 = Yarn B
3 = Yarn E
4 = Yarn F

Square 3
1 = Yarn A
2 = Yarn B
3 = Yarn G
4 = Yarn H

Square 4
1 = Yarn A
2 = Yarn B
3 = Yarn J
4 = Yarn K

Square 5
1 = Yarn A
2 = Yarn B
3 = Yarn L
4 = Yarn M

Square 6
1 = Yarn A
2 = Yarn B
3 = Yarn N
4 = Yarn P

pineapple blanket

Rowan *Colourscape* gives an extra dimension
to colorwork because of its inherent shading,
creating a brilliant, painterly effect in any
large-scale design, like the eye-catching
pineapple shapes in this big blanket.

SKILL LEVEL ◖■■■◗

FINISHED SIZE
69 x 75"/175 x 192cm

YARN
Rowan *Colourscape Chunky* (100% lambswool) [5]
4 x 3½oz/100g skeins (each approx. 175yd/160m) each in:
A – Ghost 435
3 x 3½oz/100g skeins (each approx. 175yd/160m) each in:
B – Candy Pink 434
C – Camouflage 437
2 x 3½oz/100g skeins (each approx. 175yd/160m) each in:
E – Misty 440
H – Cloud 443
1 x 3½oz/100g skein (approx. 175yd/160m) each in:
D – Spring 442
F – Storm 439
G – Frosty 433
J – Bracken 441
K – Carnival 430

NEEDLES
1 pair size 10½ (7mm) knitting needles

GAUGE
14 sts and 18 rows = 4"/10cm measured over St st using
size 10½ (7mm) needles *or size to obtain correct gauge.*

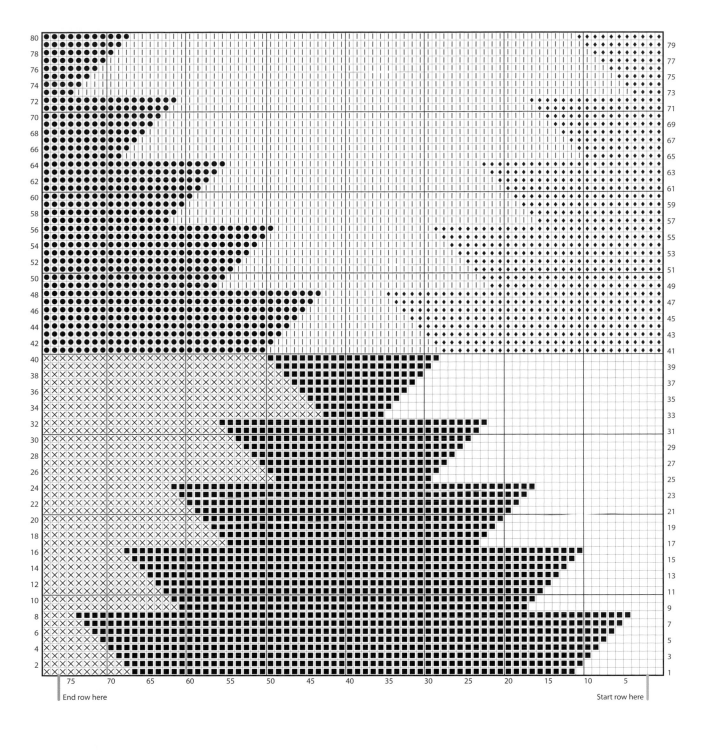

End row here

Start row here

KEY

	Color 1: Knit on RS, Purl on WS		Color 4: Knit on RS, Purl on WS
	Color 2: Knit on RS, Purl on WS		Color 5: Knit on RS, Purl on WS
	Color 3: Knit on RS, Purl on WS		Color 6: Knit on RS, Purl on WS

PATTERN NOTE
Work using the intarsia technique (see page 172).

BLANKET
Using A, cast on 230 sts.

Beg with a K row, working in St st throughout and using the intarsia technique cont as foll:

Beg and ending rows as shown, repeat chart 3 times in each row, using the colorways as shown on diagram. Work the 80 row rep as set on chart 4 times, ending with RS facing for next row.

Bind off.

CAST-ON/BOUND-OFF EDGING (both alike)
With RS facing, pick up and knit 230 sts evenly along cast-on/bound-off edge.

Work in garter st for 3"/7.5cm, AND AT SAME TIME inc 1 st at each end of every RS row.

Bind off.

EDGING
With RS facing, pick up and knit 248 sts evenly along side edge.

Work to match cast-on/bound-off edging.

Bind off.

FINISHING
Press as described on ball band.

Join corners of side and cast-on/bound-off edgings.

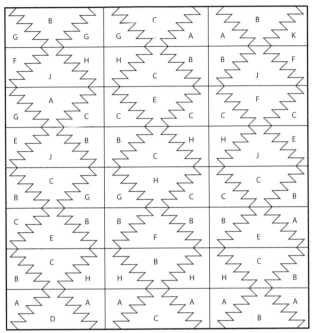

zigzag cushion

Using a mercerized cotton for this design adds a crisper outline to the zigzag stripes, giving them extra zing. I backed this cushion with one of my Rowan striped fabrics.

SKILL LEVEL ◼◼◼◻

FINISHED SIZE
15¾ x 10¼"/40 x 26cm

YARN
1 x 1¾oz/50g skein (approx. 126yd/115m) each of Rowan *Cotton Glace* (100% cotton) (2) in:
A – Twilight 829
B – Candy Floss 747
C – Blood Orange 445
D – Ochre 833
E – Heather 828
F – Whey 834

NEEDLES AND EXTRAS
1 pair size 3 (3.25mm) knitting needles
1 piece of fabric, size to match cushion plus ¾"/2cm seam allowance on all sides
Cushion form or stuffing

GAUGE
23 sts and 32 rows = 4"/10cm measured over St st using size 3 (3.25mm) needles *or size to obtain correct gauge.*

PATTERN NOTE
Work using the Fair Isle technique (see page 170).

CUSHION FRONT
Using A, cast on 91 sts.

Beg with a K row and working in St st and using the Fair Isle technique, cont as foll:
Row 1 (RS) Work 10 st rep 9 times, then work last st once.
Row 2 Work first st once, then work 10 st rep 9 times.
These 2 rows set chart placement.
Work 84 rows as set on chart, ending with RS facing for next row.
Bind off.

FINISHING
Press as described on the ball band.
Press seams. With RS facing, sew together the fabric back and knitted front with cushion form or stuffing inside.

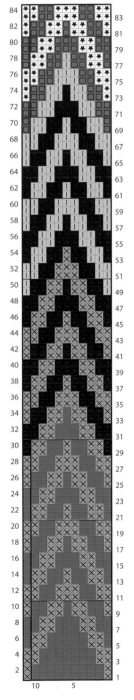

KEY

- ■ Yarn A: Knit on RS, Purl on WS
- ⊠ Yarn B: Knit on RS, Purl on WS
- ■ Yarn C: Knit on RS, Purl on WS
- | Yarn D: Knit on RS, Purl on WS
- ▣ Yarn E: Knit on RS, Purl on WS
- ✳ Yarn F: Knit on RS, Purl on WS

triangle cushion

I love the way this cushion makes the best use of a terrific range of colors, making it so vibrant and organic in feel, while using the darker shades for the bottom triangle in each square "grounds" the design.

SKILL LEVEL ◖■■■▭

FINISHED SIZE
17 x 13½"/43 x 34cm

YARN
1 x 1¾oz/50g skein (approx. 126yd/115m) each of Rowan *Cotton Glace* (100% cotton) (2) in:
A – Twilight 829
B – Chalk 827
C – Heather 828
D – Bubbles 724
E – Dijon 739
F – Ochre 833
G – Sky 749
H – Dawn Grey 831
J – Baked Red 837
K – Persimmon 832
L – Ivy 812
M – Whey 834
N – Blood Orange 445
P – Umber 838

NEEDLES AND EXTRAS
1 pair size 3 (3.25mm) knitting needles
1 piece of fabric, size to match cushion plus ¾"/2cm seam allowance on all sides
Cushion form or stuffing

GAUGE
23 sts and 32 rows = 4"/10cm measured over St st using size 3 (3.25mm) needles *or size to obtain correct gauge.*

CUSHION
FRONT
Using A, cast on 100 sts.
Working 10 sts as set on chart 10 times, using the colors as shown as the color layout diagram, cont from chart until all the color blocks shown on the diagram have been worked, ending with RS facing for next row.
Bind off.

FINISHING
Press as described on the ball band.
Press seams. With RS facing, sew together the fabric back and knitted front with cushion form or stuffing inside.

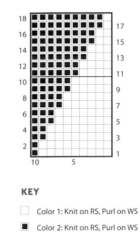

18 · 17
16 · 15
14 · 13
12 · 11
10 · 9
8 · 7
6 · 5
4 · 3
2 · 1
10 · 5

KEY

☐ Color 1: Knit on RS, Purl on WS

■ Color 2: Knit on RS, Purl on WS

COLOR LAYOUT DIAGRAM

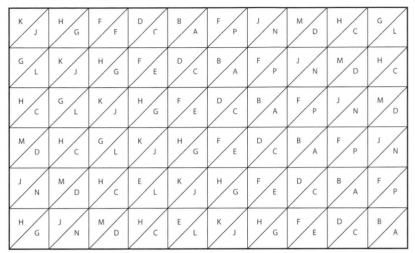

K/J	H/G	F/F	D/C	B/A	F/P	J/N	M/D	H/C	G/L
G/L	K/J	H/G	F/E	D/C	B/A	F/P	J/N	M/D	H/C
H/C	G/L	K/J	H/G	F/E	D/C	B/A	F/P	J/N	M/D
M/D	H/C	G/L	K/J	H/G	F/E	D/C	B/A	F/P	J/N
J/N	M/D	H/C	E/L	K/J	H/G	F/E	D/C	B/A	F/P
H/G	J/N	M/D	H/C	E/L	K/J	H/G	F/E	D/C	B/A

half-circle throw

I think this design is fun. I love the way the color choices change the way you "view" the circles, giving it a life of its own. Rowan *Handknit Cotton* is softer and thicker than *Cotton Glace*, so is a good choice for a bigger item like a throw.

SKILL LEVEL

FINISHED SIZE
53 x 67¾"/134 x 172cm

YARN
Rowan *Handknit Cotton* (100% cotton) (4)
3 x 1¾oz/50g skeins (each approx. 93yd/85m) each in:
A – Delphinium 334
H – Burnt 343
2 x 1¾oz/50g skeins (each approx. 93yd/85m) each in:
B – Slick 313
C – Ice Water 239
D – Tangerine Dream 337
E – Celery 309
F – Sunflower 336
G – Turkish Plum 277
J – Cloud 345
K – Raffia 330

NEEDLES
1 size 7 (4.5mm) circular knitting needle
1 pair size 7 (4.5mm) knitting needles

GAUGE
19 sts and 27 rows = 4"/10cm measured over St st using size 7 (4.5mm) needles *or size to obtain correct gauge*.

THROW

Using A and size 7 (4.5mm) circular needle, cast on 242 sts.
Working back and forth, cont as foll:
Knit 8 rows.
Beg with a K row, working in St st throughout, beg and ending rows as shown and working center 30 st rep 8 times, working 28 row rep throughout in colorways as shown on diagram, cont as set until 448 rows have been worked (16 bands of patt), ending after 7th band of pattern and with RS

facing for next row.
Using A, knit 7 rows.
Bind off knitwise on WS.

SIDE EDGINGS (both alike)
Using size 7 (4.5mm)
needles and A, cast on 8 sts.
Work in garter st until band
fits up side edge, sewing in
place at same time.
Bind off.
Press as described on the
ball band.

CHART CONTINUED

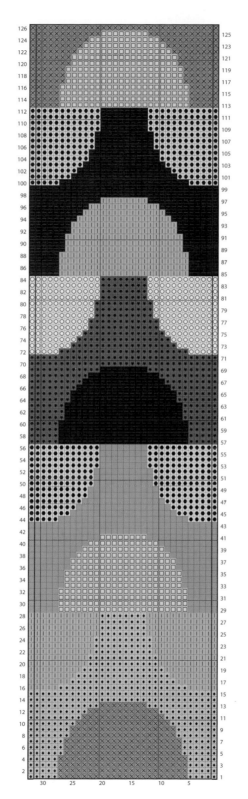

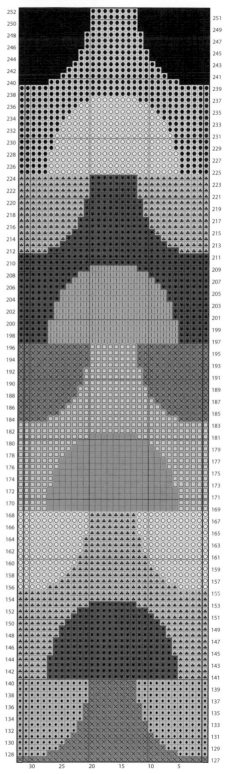

KEY

- Yarn A: K on RS, P on WS
- Yarn B: K on RS, P on WS
- Yarn C: K on RS, P on WS
- Yarn D: K on RS, P on WS
- Yarn E: K on RS, P on WS
- Yarn F: K on RS, P on WS
- Yarn G: K on RS, P on WS
- Yarn H: K on RS, P on WS
- Yarn J: K on RS, P on WS
- Yarn K: K on RS, P on WS
- Pattern repeat

broken stripe scarf

Rowan *Pure Wool 4 ply* has an extensive color range, so you can find plenty of inspiring hues to choose from.

SKILL LEVEL ◖■□□▹

FINISHED SIZE
12½ x 66"/32 x 168cm

YARN
1 x 1¾oz/50g skein (approx. 175yd/160m) each of Rowan *Pure Wool 4 ply* (100% superwash wool) 🧶**1** in:

A – Port 437

B – Black 404

C – Shale 402

D – Kiss 436

E – Blue Iris 455

F – Mocha 417

G – Eau de Nil 450

H – Sage 448

J – Quarry Tile 457

K – Navy 411

L – Framboise 456

M – Hyacinth 426

N – Havanna 458

P – Avocado 419

NEEDLES
1 pair size 3 (3.25mm) knitting needles

GAUGE
28 sts and 36 rows = 4"/10cm measured over St st using size 3 (3.25mm) needles *or size to obtain correct gauge.*

SCARF
Using A, cast on 90 sts.
Knit 6 rows.
Next row (RS) With A K5, knit next 80 sts as set on chart, K5 with A.
Next row (WS) With A K5, purl next 80 sts as set on chart, K5 with A.
These 2 rows set chart placement, St st over center sts and garter st on edge sts.
Cont as set, working the 120-row patt rep thoughout until scarf measures 65½"/166cm, ending with RS facing for next row.
Using A, knit 7 rows.
Bind off knitwise on WS.
Press as described on the ball band.

KEY

- 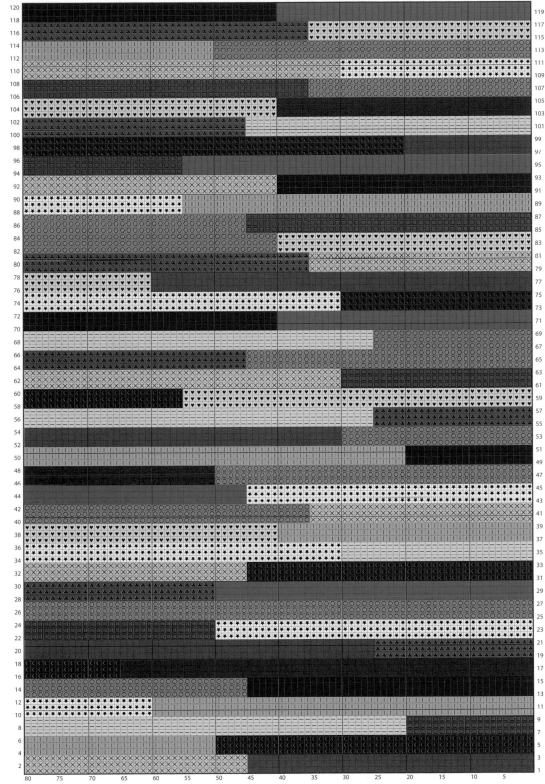 Yarn A: Knit on RS, Purl on WS
- Yarn B: Knit on RS, Purl on WS
- Yarn C: Knit on RS, Purl on WS
- Yarn D: Knit on RS, Purl on WS
- Yarn E: Knit on RS, Purl on WS
- Yarn F: Knit on RS, Purl on WS
- Yarn G: Knit on RS, Purl on WS
- Yarn H: Knit on RS, Purl on WS
- Yarn J: Knit on RS, Purl on WS
- Yarn K: Knit on RS, Purl on WS
- Yarn L: Knit on RS, Purl on WS
- Yarn M: Knit on RS, Purl on WS
- Yarn N: Knit on RS, Purl on WS
- Yarn P: Knit on RS, Purl on WS
- Pattern repeat

multistripe cushion

This cushion has a really neat geometric design, right down to the borders where the stripes run vertically. *Cotton Glace* helps the colors to really sing out against each other.

SKILL LEVEL ⬤▬▬▬▬

FINISHED SIZE
20½ x 16"/52 x 41cm

YARN
Rowan *Cotton Glace* (100% cotton) 🔲2
1 x 1¾oz/50g skein (approx. 126yd/115m) each in:
D – Baked Red 837
F – Umber 838
G – Candy Floss 747
J – Shoot 814
K – Ecru 723
2 x 1¾oz/50g skein (approx. 126yd/115m) each in:
A – Poppy 741
B – Bubbles 724
H – Garnet 841
1 x 1¾oz/50g skein (approx. 153yd/140m) of Rowan *Siena*
(100% cotton) 🔲1 each in:
C – Greengage 661
E – Pacific 660

NEEDLES AND EXTRAS
1 pair size 2/3 (3mm) needles
1 pair size 2 (2.75mm) needles
Cushion form or stuffing

GAUGE
28 sts and 38 rows = 4"/10cm measured over St st using
size 2/3 (3mm) needles *or size to obtain correct gauge.*

FRONT
Using A, cast on 146 sts.
Beg with a K row and working in St st throughout, cont in patt as set on chart until all 156 rows have been completed.
Using A, bind off.

BACK
Using A, cast on 146 sts.
Beg with a K row, working in St st and stripe rep of 14 rows A, then 14 rows B, cont for 154 rows (11 bands of color).
Work 2 rows in A. Bind off.

FINISHING
Press as described on the ball band.
With RS facing, sew together the knitted back and front with cushion pad or stuffing inside.

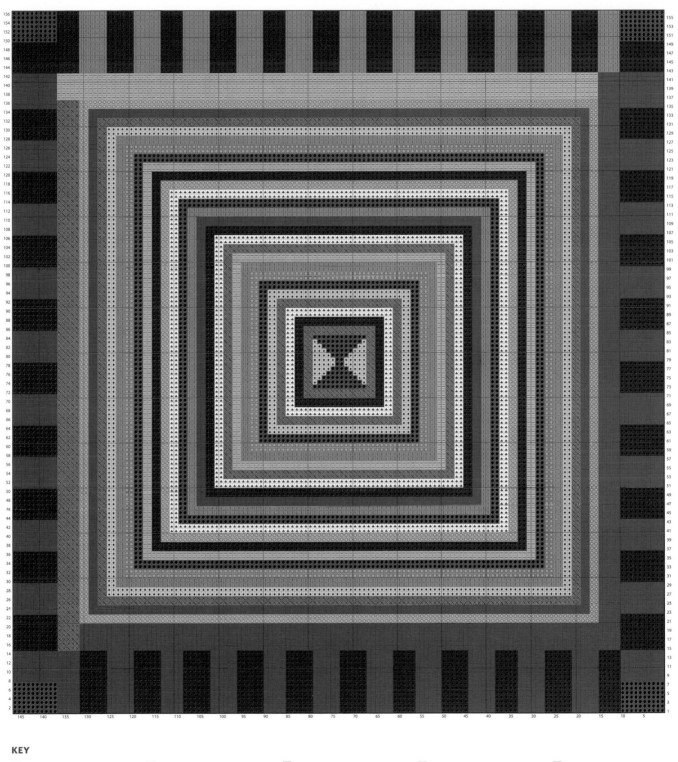

KEY

- ■ Yarn A: Knit on RS, Purl on WS
- ◆ Yarn C: Knit on RS, Purl on WS
- ▢ Yarn E: Knit on RS, Purl on WS
- ■ Yarn G: Knit on RS, Purl on WS
- ■ Yarn J: Knit on RS, Purl on WS
- ■ Yarn B: Knit on RS, Purl on WS
- ■ Yarn D: Knit on RS, Purl on WS
- ■ Yarn F: Knit on RS, Purl on WS
- ■ Yarn H: Knit on RS, Purl on WS
- ♣ Yarn K: Knit on RS, Purl on WS

moody hues

Here we find the colors of old tapestries or ethnic wraps that have seen a lot of wear, resulting in faded, stonewashed textures. Brandon has produced a set of random cushions in chalky tones of *Summer Tweed*, with a gentle smattering of dots inspired by aboriginal painted poles in Australia. His colorways show how a simple design changes mood when done in lighter or darker tones. The half-circle appears here again, transformed into a deep romantic coloring, almost unrecognizably connected to the pastel throw in the previous chapter yet the same pattern (see page 58). These smoldering hues are so flattering and mysterious when worn. The triangles of our "stone cushions" feature a very natural palette of stone and wood tones. The strong geometry is softened by rows of contrast colors—they look great with old textiles. The trapezoid throw is probably my favorite knit in this book—the yarn has a delicious feel as it slips between your fingers, and the geometric pattern is easy to memorize and just flows along.

x-factor blanket

Every once in a while a friend who is computer savvy (which I am not) will alert me to some gorgeous piece of design on eBay. A silk patchwork quilt made in the 1800s came up, and the powerful graphic of it in a brilliant palette leapt out at me. I bought it at once and did a quiet version of it for my book *Quilts en Provence*. Making it, I realized the large patterns were created entirely from simple blocks of diagonal stripes. "What a good idea for a knit," I thought, and got a friend of mine to help knit blocks for the blanket. The gorgeous colors of *Summer Tweed* were perfect for the effect I was after. I love the way these diagonal squares add up to such dynamic "Xs." It would be thrilling to see this blanket in other moods—perhaps cobalt, purple, turquoise, and Kelly greens with maroons, black, and navy for contrasts.

SEE PAGE 106 FOR PATTERN.

OPPOSITE A detail of the blanket against the exciting backdrop of a big painting of Chinese ancestors in our living room. The geometry of the painting mirrors the geometry of the blanket brilliantly.
BELOW LEFT The quilt that inspired the blanket.
BELOW CENTER AND RIGHT Brandon and me at the photo shoot. We loved the way the tiles echoed the geometry.
OVERLEAF The colors in the X-factor blanket work beautifully with some of our tapestry cushions.

dotty cushions

The simple repeats of Brandon's dotty cushions just cry out for several versions in different colors. Brandon explains his inspiration: "I don't know what it is, but I'm just crazy about dots and spots, from aboriginal paintings to animal markings. I find myself using a lot of dot motifs in my artwork for fabric designs on my cushions. Each dot on these cushions has its own shape and size, giving the design a random intrigue and playfulness. Working several color combinations in the same pattern should encourage you to play with your own combos. These are knitted in Rowan's *Summer Tweed* (a silk and linen blend). Modern and cheeky, they would look cozy on an old leather couch or sharp and stylish in a minimal setting. Both Kaffe and I were charmed to see how they worked against this old terracotta brick wall wedged behind an early budding apple blossom tree."

SEE PAGE 110 FOR PATTERN.

LEFT This weather-worn terracotta wall and espaliered tree give the playful dotty cushions a fun setting. RIGHT They also look great pattern-on-pattern, seen here on the dapple patchwork print on our living room chairs.

amish blanket

I saw a fabulous Amish quilt that was nothing but large panels of diagonal stripes. I was so taken by it that I had to knit it. It took a while to complete, but each panel went faster and faster as I got used to the repetition of the diagonal stripes in mostly two colors. Bringing in the odd kick of a third color was fun and spicy.

There is a great satisfaction in knitting a big project like this as you stack up panel after panel. I arrange mine on a work wall of gray flannel that I use for patchwork. It's a good ground to put any color combo on while working on it, as it helps you assess what is needed next.

It goes without saying that this could be done in many different moods. There is a golden ochre in this color combo, but imagine if you replaced that with a soft red and had dark maroons, navy, browns, and lavenders. What a totally different, rich effect that would create.

SEE PAGE 112 FOR PATTERN.

LEFT The simple diagonal stripes in the Amish blanket create a fabulous ripple of movement.
RIGHT Seen in close-up on an Arts and Crafts bed, the throw goes well with the dotty cushions and the stone triangles cushion.

colorscape stripe scarf

Taking two of the colorscape colorways and alternating them every eighth row is a very exciting knitting adventure indeed. The most novice of knitters can shine after producing this totally easy-to-knit stole. I picked two gray-based palettes with just enough difference to create low contrast. You could go for a bolder look by taking a very dark skein and running it with a much lighter, brighter skein or colorway.

I hope you enjoy this scarf as much as I did. Seeing what color pops up next to the one just knitted keeps you constantly motivated to move along. SEE PAGE 116 FOR PATTERN.

OPPOSITE I love the way the colors in the stripes of this scarf shift into a brighter gear at one end. The tones pick up those of the fabulous Moorcroft pot on the Arts and Crafts cabinet.
BELOW The colorscape scarf stripes (left) mirror the rows of old terracotta pots on dark earth (right).

stone triangles cushion

LEFT AND BELOW The dusky neutral colors of the triangle cushion echo those in the old watering can, silvered wood, and unusual hellebore bloom.

I love knitting the same structure in different colors to see how it changes—I've enlarged the scale from the triangle cushion in the last chapter (see page 57). Using thicker yarn and larger needles has made a bolder look, while the colors are more muted. It reminds me of the pebbles on a beach, all tones of gray.

Someone once asked me, "If you could only work with one color, what would it be?" I thought for a second, then said "Gray." I pictured the rich variety of colors one sees on a beach—pinks, greens, blues, and golds, all with gray overtones. If I'd chosen the obvious cobalt blue, scarlet, or emerald green, I'd soon be bored with just the one color, but grays have been in my knitting palette for years, and I never tire of their subtle tones.

This cushion looks so handsome paired with old textiles. It could be equally great in a modern, steel gray interior. I can also imagine it as a big patchwork throw for a couch, made of multiples of the cushion sewn together. It would look very African.

SEE PAGE 118 FOR PATTERN.

earthy zigzag cushion

This is another example of the magic of enlarging a charted design by knitting it with thicker yarns on larger needles. These smoldering earthy tones are shown to advantage by the zigzag layout. How different from the fine *Cotton Glace* version on page 54. These big yarns could be great for a knitted afghan to nap under. Alternatively, try the zigzags in a sampler, featuring squares of most of the motifs in this book—the shadowboxes, half-circles, triangles, checkerboards, dots, and pineapples from this and earlier chapters, along with the wiggles, red circles, and trapezoids to come. You could knit the squares separately in a chunky yarn. Crochet borders around them before sewing together (that way you could even up any discrepancy in size by adding a double or triple border where needed). I'd love to see the results! You could make a set of cushions using other colors: try wine reds with ochre and purple, or grays with stony greens, blues, and pinks.

SEE PAGE 122 FOR PATTERN.

LEFT AND RIGHT The vintage tiles and plates inspired the mood of the earthy zigzag cushion, which looks perfect on a cut-velvet chair.

trapezoid throw

This is far and away my favorite design in this book for sheer ease of knitting and great results. You simply start with blocks of color and move all of them one stitch to the right for fifteen rows, then change to a new set of colors and knit blocks one stitch to the left for the next fifteen rows. As you repeat this easily remembered formula, a jaunty pattern emerges that really is eye-catching.

The gorgeous silky yarn is a pleasure to knit with and cozy to wrap up in. I see this as a handsome throw for the end of a couch, great to snuggle under while watching TV.

I used most of the color range in this throw, but you could concentrate on just the warm reds and purples or cooler greens, blues, and grays. See how different it looks in the neat small stitches of *Cotton Glace* as our next project (see page 102).

SEE PAGE 124 FOR PATTERN.

RIGHT This detail shows the easy-to-knit trapezoid shapes of this textured throw.

OPPOSITE The muted green paint and weathered doors set off the distinctive palette of our throw.

trapezoid cushion

Here, I've picked a slightly brighter palette in silky *Cotton Glace* yarns. Compared to the trapezoid throw, they are knitted on much smaller needles so the scale is quite reduced, which makes it appear even pointier to me. I've used a rich, medium-tone palette with quite a low contrast. Imagine it in really sharp contrast: black with white and scarlet or yellow, ochre, and peat browns, navy, and Bordeaux, for a look as eye catching as a road sign to jazz up a couch or chair; or try the opposite, quiet tones of opals, grays, pinks, baby blue, and so on. Perhaps cream, white, pale pastels like Brandon's baby blanket on page 16.

SEE PAGE 128 FOR PATTERN.

BELOW AND RIGHT Our tiled terrace, with the mosaic garden pots we made for London's Chelsea Flower Show. The finer *Cotton Glace* version of the trapezoid pattern is enhanced by this rich mosaic.

hyacinth scarf

This soft coloring is achieved by running one of my sock yarns along with a thread of *Kidsilk Haze*. The *Kidsilk* softens the bright sock yarn, creating a misty effect.

This is a great way of making color just a bit more atmospheric and mysterious. As a painter, I often apply a layer of transparent glaze—a color that is so liquid it can be seen through—to my colors when I want them to be lighter and more luminous, or softened down to recede a little. The great mural painter Maxfield Parrish, who was famous for the depth of his blue skies, would put a wash of red over cobalt blue to deepen the effect.

The other day I tried a sock yarn that was mostly ochre and ran it with blood-red *Kidsilk Haze*. The effect was so warm and rich that I'm planning a big project in it soon.

Try combinations of your own. Strange ones like green with red or maroon with purple. If you want to make a blue bluer, add a deeper blue haze to it.

SEE PAGE 132 FOR PATTERN.

LEFT How well this scarf goes with neutral grays and with navy and white. RIGHT Here you get the full impact of the fine gradations of color and yarn.

x-factor blanket

The rich, yet soft, colors of Rowan *Summer Tweed* turn this showstopping pattern into a real work of art. Echoing the stripes in the border adds to the richness of it, as you can see in the photo on the opposite page.

SKILL LEVEL ■■■■

FINISHED SIZE
Each square to measure approx. 10¼ x 6¾"/26 x 17cm

YARN
Rowan *Summer Tweed* (70% silk; 30% cotton) (4)
1 x 1¾oz/50g skein (approx. 131yd/120m) each in:
A – Brilliant 528
C – Blueberry 525
Q – Toast 530
R – Raffia 515
S – Sunset 509
U – Harbour 549
V – Jardinier 544
2 x 1¾oz/50g skeins (each approx. 131yd/120m) in:
B – Denim 529
E – Bamboo 552
F – Powder 500
G – Loganberry 546
H – Butterball 538
J – Torrid 536
K – Reed 514
L – Mango 542
N – Rush 507
P – Tonic 551
T – Summer Berry 537

3 x 1¾oz/50g skeins (each approx. 131yd/120m) in:
D – Navy 547
M – Smoulder 522

NEEDLES
1 pair size 8 (5mm) knitting needles
1 size 7 (4.5mm) crochet hook

GAUGE
16 sts and 23 rows = 4"/10cm measured over St st using size 8 (5mm) needles *or size to obtain correct gauge.*

PATTERN NOTE
Work using the intarsia technique (see page 172).

BLANKET SQUARES (make 48)
Using appropriate color, cast on 42 sts.
Beg with a K row and working in St st, beg and ending rows as indicated and using the intarsia technique, work 38 rows as set on appropriate chart using the colors as listed.

FINISHING
Join squares together as shown in diagram, rotating if necessary to create diamond shapes.

STRIPED EDGINGS (work 4 alike)
Cast on 14 sts.
Beg with a K row, working in St st and a stripe pattern of your choice (version shown uses mostly P and J with hints of other colors) but keeping each stripe 10 rows deep, cont as foll:
Row 1 (RS) Knit to last st, slip last st, k1 from edge of throw then psso.
Row 2 Purl.
Cont as set until edging fits along 1 edge of throw.
Bind off.

CORNER SQUARES

(make 4)

Using K, cast on 14 sts.
Beg with a K row and
working in St st throughout,
using intarsia technique
work 16 rows as set on
chart B.
Bind off.
Sew corner squares in
place at ends of striped
edgings.

CROCHET EDGING

Using size 7 (4.5mm)
crochet hook and P, work
1 round single crochet all
round edge of throw, slip
stitch to join.
Next round Using G, work
2 ch, work 1 round single
crochet all round edge of
throw, slip stitch to join.
Next round Using D, work
2 ch, work 1 round single
crochet all round edge of
throw, slip stitch to join.
Fasten off.

dotty cushions

The soft colors of this yarn coupled with the eye-catching design creates a wonderful series of four colorways for this charming cushion. You could quite easily adapt it to make a good stole by carrying on with the repeat.

SKILL LEVEL ◼◼◻◻◻

FINISHED SIZE
19¾ x 19¾"/50 x 50cm

YARN
Rowan *Summer Tweed* (70% silk; 30% cotton)
2 x 1¾oz/50g skeins (each approx. 131yd/120m) each in A;
1 x 1¾oz/50g skein in B
Shown in following colorways:
A – Tonic 551, Loganberry 546, Jardinier 544, Summer Berry 537
B – Torrid 536, Powder 500, Raffia 515, Navy 547

NEEDLES AND EXTRAS
1 pair size 8 (5mm) knitting needles
1 piece of fabric, size to match cushion plus ¾"/2cm seam allowance on all sides
Cushion form or stuffing

GAUGE
16 sts and 23 rows = 4"/10cm measured over St st using size 8 (5mm) needles *or size to obtain correct gauge.*

FRONT
Using A, cast on 80 sts.
Beg with a K row, working in St st and using the intarsia technique, working the 40 row rep as set on chart throughout, cont until work measures 19¾"/50cm, ending with RS facing for next row.
Using A, bind off.

FINISHING
Press as described on the ball band.
Press seams. With RS facing, sew together the fabric back and knitted front with cushion form or stuffing inside.

KEY

☐ Yarn A: Knit on RS, Purl on WS

■ Yarn B: Knit on RS, Purl on WS

☐ Pattern repeat

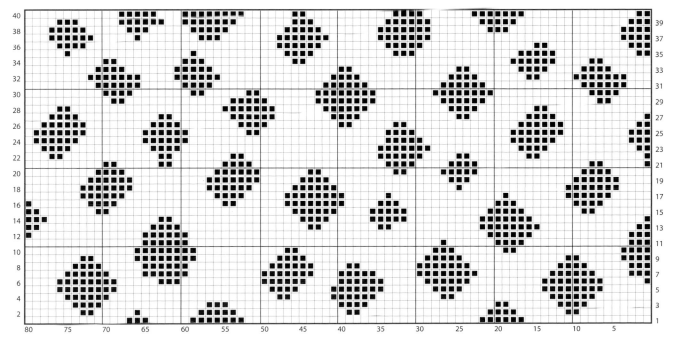

SQUARE LAYOUT DIAGRAM

15	14	13
12	11	10
9	8	7
6	5	4
3	2	1

Square 1

1 – Yarn A
2 – Yarn B
3 – Yarn A
4 – Yarn B
5 – Yarn A
6 – Yarn B
7 – Yarn A
8 – Yarn B
9 – Yarn A
10 – Yarn B
11 – Yarn C
12 – Yarn B
13 – Yarn D
14 – Yarn E
15 – Yarn F
16 – Yarn B
17 – Yarn A

Square 2
(sewn upside down)

1 – Yarn C
2 – Yarn E
3 – Yarn C
4 – Yarn G
5 – Yarn H
6 – Yarn E
7 – Yarn J
8 – Yarn E
9 – Yarn C
10 – Yarn G
11 – Yarn C
12 – Yarn L
13 – Yarn C
14 – Yarn E
15 – Yarn J
16 – Yarn E
17 – Yarn A

Square 3

1 – Yarn N

2 – Yarn M
3 – Yarn L
4 – Yarn M
5 – Yarn L
6 – Yarn M
7 – Yarn L
8 – Yarn M
9 – Yarn N
10 – Yarn M
11 – Yarn L
12 – Yarn E
13 – Yarn L
14 – Yarn M
15 – Yarn N
16 – Yarn M
17 – Yarn L

Square 4

1 – Yarn M
2 – Yarn F
3 – Yarn M
4 – Yarn D
5 – Yarn M
6 – Yarn P
7 – Yarn M
8 – Yarn Q
9 – Yarn M
10 – Yarn D
11 – Yarn M
12 – Yarn P
13 – Yarn M
14 – Yarn F
15 – Yarn M
16 – Yarn Q
17 – Yarn M

Square 5

1 – Yarn G
2 – Yarn P
3 – Yarn G
4 – Yarn P
5 – Yarn G

6 – Yarn P
7 – Yarn G
8 – Yarn P
9 – Yarn G
10 – Yarn P
11 – Yarn G
12 – Yarn P
13 – Yarn G
14 – Yarn D
15 – Yarn G
16 – Yarn P
17 – Yarn G

Square 6

1 – Yarn Q
2 – Yarn K
3 – Yarn R
4 – Yarn Q
5 – Yarn K
6 – Yarn G
7 – Yarn Q
8 – Yarn K
9 – Yarn R
10 – Yarn Q
11 – Yarn J
12 – Yarn G
13 – Yarn Q
14 – Yarn K
15 – Yarn G
16 – Yarn Q
17 – Yarn H

Square 7

1 – Yarn K
2 – Yarn P
3 – Yarn K
4 – Yarn P
5 – Yarn K
6 – Yarn P
7 – Yarn K
8 – Yarn P
9 – Yarn K

10 – Yarn P
11 – Yarn K
12 – Yarn Q
13 – Yarn K
14 – Yarn P
15 – Yarn K
16 – Yarn D
17 – Yarn K

Square 8
(sewn upside down)

1 – Yarn E
2 – Yarn L
3 – Yarn E
4 – Yarn S
5 – Yarn E
6 – Yarn Q
7 – Yarn E
8 – Yarn S
9 – Yarn E
10 – Yarn L
11 – Yarn E
12 – Yarn L
13 – Yarn E
14 – Yarn S
15 – Yarn B
16 – Yarn L
17 – Yarn E

Square 9
(sewn upside down)

1 – Yarn K
2 – Yarn B
3 – Yarn K
4 – Yarn B
5 – Yarn K
6 – Yarn B
7 – Yarn K
8 – Yarn B
9 – Yarn K

10 – Yarn G
11 – Yarn K
12 – Yarn B
13 – Yarn A
14 – Yarn B
15 – Yarn K
16 – Yarn B
17 – Yarn K

Square 10
(sewn upside down)

1 – Yarn L
2 – Yarn A
3 – Yarn L
4 – Yarn H
5 – Yarn L
6 – Yarn A
7 – Yarn L
8 – Yarn A
9 – Yarn L
10 – Yarn K
11 – Yarn L
12 – Yarn A
13 – Yarn L
14 – Yarn A
15 – Yarn L
16 – Yarn D
17 – Yarn L

Square 11

1 – Yarn G
2 – Yarn H
3 – Yarn G
4 – Yarn A
5 – Yarn G
6 – Yarn A
7 – Yarn G
8 – Yarn A
9 – Yarn G
10 – Yarn A
11 – Yarn G

12 – Yarn A
13 – Yarn E
14 – Yarn A
15 – Yarn G
16 – Yarn A
17 – Yarn G

Square 12

1 – Yarn R
2 – Yarn D
3 – Yarn R
4 – Yarn F
5 – Yarn R
6 – Yarn F
7 – Yarn R
8 – Yarn F
9 – Yarn R
10 – Yarn D
11 – Yarn R
12 – Yarn F
13 – Yarn R
14 – Yarn P
15 – Yarn R
16 – Yarn F
17 – Yarn R

Square 13
(sewn upside down)

1 – Yarn B
2 – Yarn D
3 – Yarn E
4 – Yarn D
5 – Yarn G
6 – Yarn A
7 – Yarn G
8 – Yarn J
9 – Yarn G
10 – Yarn P
11 – Yarn E
12 – Yarn D
13 – Yarn E

14 – Yarn F
15 – Yarn H
16 – Yarn D
17 – Yarn E

Square 14

1 – Yarn H
2 – Yarn L
3 – Yarn H
4 – Yarn S
5 – Yarn H
6 – Yarn L
7 – Yarn H
8 – Yarn S
9 – Yarn H
10 – Yarn S
11 – Yarn H
12 – Yarn M
13 – Yarn H
14 – Yarn L
15 – Yarn H
16 – Yarn L
17 – Yarn H

Square 15

1 – Yarn M
2 – Yarn K
3 – Yarn M
4 – Yarn K
5 – Yarn E
6 – Yarn K
7 – Yarn M
8 – Yarn K
9 – Yarn M
10 – Yarn K
11 – Yarn M
12 – Yarn K
13 – Yarn M
14 – Yarn K
15 – Yarn M
16 – Yarn K
17 – Yarn M

colorscape stripe scarf

The fun of this design is that most of the striping is inherent in the yarn itself (in two colorways).

SKILL LEVEL ◼◼◻◻

FINISHED SIZE
10¾ x 62¼"/27 x 158cm)

YARN
1 x 3½oz/100g skein (approx. 175yd/160m) each of Rowan *Colourscape Chunky* (100% lambswool) ⑤ in:
A – Storm 439
B – Bracken 441

NEEDLES
1 pair size 10 (6mm) knitting needles

GAUGE
15 sts and 21 rows = 4"/10cm measured over St st using size 10 (6mm) needles *or size to obtain correct gauge.*

SCARF
Before knitting, ensure you begin with a pale-colored section of each yarn.
Using A, cast on 40 sts.
Knit 2 rows.
Row 1 (RS) Knit.
Row 2 K2, P to last 2 sts, k2.
These 2 rows set St st and garter st edges.
Cont as set working 4 rows more in A, then in stripe patt of 8 rows B, 8 rows A until scarf measures approx. 62"/157cm, ending after 7 rows of B.
Knit 2 rows in B.
Bind off knitwise on WS in B.

stone triangles cushion

This version of the triangle design is satisfyingly quick to knit in a thick yet soft yarn like Rowan *Felted Tweed Aran*. Back it with one of the Rowan striped fabrics for best effect. It has our trademark simple striped borders (see page 121).

SKILL LEVEL ◖■■■▱

FINISHED SIZE
18 x 19"/46 x 49cm

YARN
1 x 1¾oz/50g skein (each approx. 95yd/87m) each of Rowan *Felted Tweed Aran* (50% merino wool; 25% alpaca; 25% viscose) (4) in:
A – Heather 724
B – Dusty 728
C – Plum 731
D – Burnt 722
E – Soot 729
F – Sage 726
G – Cassis 723
H – Cork 721
J – Teal 725
K – Storm Blue 730
L – Pebble 720

NEEDLES AND EXTRAS
1 pair size 8 (5mm) knitting needles
1 size 8 (5mm) circular knitting needle
1 piece of fabric, size to match cushion plus ¾"/2cm seam allowance on all sides
Cushion form or stuffing

Yarn A: Knit on RS, Purl on WS

Yarn B: Knit on RS, Purl on WS

Yarn C: Knit on RS, Purl on WS

Yarn D: Knit on RS, Purl on WS

Yarn E: Knit on RS, Purl on WS

Yarn F: Knit on RS, Purl on WS

Yarn G: Knit on RS, Purl on WS

Yarn H: Knit on RS, Purl on WS

Yarn J: Knit on RS, Purl on WS

Yarn K: Knit on RS, Purl on WS

Yarn L: Knit on RS, Purl on WS

GAUGE

16 sts and 23 rows = 4"/10cm measured over St st using size 8 (5mm) needles *or size to obtain correct gauge.*

CUSHION
FRONT

Using A, cast on 60 sts.

Working 10 sts as set on chart 6 times and using the colors as shown in chart until all the color blocks have been worked, ending with RS facing for next row.

Bind off.

EDGING

With RS facing, using size 8 (5mm) circular needle, starting in center of cast-on edge, pick up and knit 10 sts in F from 1st color block, 10 sts in E from 2nd color block, 10 sts in F from 3rd color block, 1 st in E from corner, 10 sts in F from next color block. Cont in this way, alternating the colors, until you have worked all round the edge of the cushion. *224 sts.*

Working in St st and rows not rounds, using the intarsia technique, work to corner st, M1 using same color as corner st, k1, M1 using same color as corner st, cont in this way to end. *232 sts.*

Work 1 row.

Next round Work to corner st, M1 using same color as corner st, k3, M1 using same color as corner st, cont in this way to end. *240 sts.*

Cont in this way, increasing 2 st at each corner of 6 foll alt rows. *264 sts.*

Bind off.

FINISHING

Press as described on the ball band.

Press seams and with RS facing sew together the fabric back and knitted front with cushion form or stuffing inside.

earthy zigzag cushion

When you knit this design in a soft yarn like Rowan *Cocoon*, it gives an entirely new look to the zigzag pattern, softening the inherent color contrasts.

SKILL LEVEL ◼◼◼◻

FINISHED SIZE
14 x 13"/36 x 34cm

YARN
1 x 3½oz/100g skein (approx. 126yd/115m) each of Rowan *Cocoon* (80% merino wool; 20% kid mohair) (5) in:

A – Seascape 813
B – Amber 815
C – Kiwi 816
D – Quarry Tile 818
E – Crag 809
F – Tundra 808
G – Mountain 805
H – Petal 823

NEEDLES AND EXTRAS
1 pair size 10½ (6.5mm) knitting needles
1 piece of fabric, size to match cushion plus ¾"/2cm seam allowance on sides
Cushion form or stuffing

GAUGE
16 sts and 18 rows = 4"/10cm measured over St st using size 10.5 (6.5mm) needles *or size to obtain correct gauge.*

FRONT
Using size 10½ (6.5mm) needles and A, cast on 57 sts.
Beg with a K row and working in St st throughout, cont as foll:

Beg and ending rows as indicated and using the Fair Isle technique (see page 170), work 60 rows as set on chart, ending with RS facing for next row.
Bind off.

FINISHING
Press as described on the ball band.
Press seams. With RS facing, sew together the fabric back and knitted front with cushion form or stuffing inside.

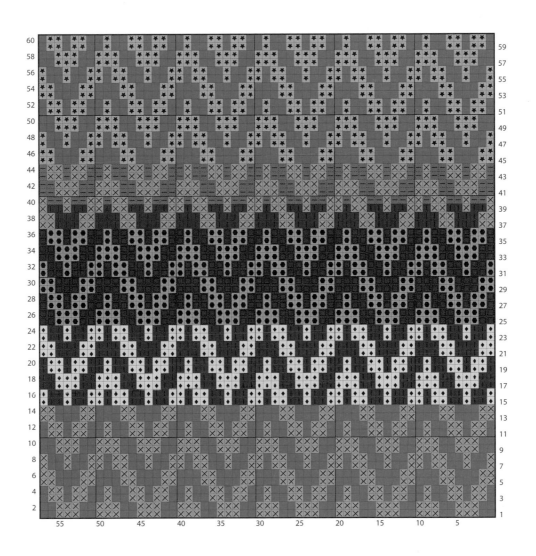

KEY

- Yarn A: Knit on RS, Purl on WS
- Yarn B: Knit on RS, Purl on WS
- Yarn C: Knit on RS, Purl on WS
- Yarn D: Knit on RS, Purl on WS
- Yarn E: Knit on RS, Purl on WS
- Yarn F: Knit on RS, Purl on WS
- Yarn G: Knit on RS, Purl on WS
- Yarn H: Knit on RS, Purl on WS

trapezoid throw

This throw is knitted using the intarsia technique (see page 172) in Rowan *Kidsilk Aura*, which is a thicker version of the more well-known *Kidsilk Haze*, but you can easily knit the colors in Rowan *Kidsilk Haze* held double, if you wish.

KEY

☐ Color 1: Knit on RS, Purl on WS
■ Color 2: Knit on RS, Purl on WS
☒ Color 3: Knit on RS, Purl on WS
◆ Color 4: Knit on RS, Purl on WS
⦙ Color 5: Knit on RS, Purl on WS
● Color 6: Knit on RS, Purl on WS
☐ Color 7: Knit on RS, Purl on WS
◉ Color 8: Knit on RS, Purl on WS
— Color 9: Knit on RS, Purl on WS
✱ Color 10: Knit on RS, Purl on WS
○ Color 11: Knit on RS, Purl on WS
♣ Color 12: Knit on RS, Purl on WS

SKILL LEVEL

FINISHED SIZE

51½ x 67¾"/131 x 172cm

YARN

Rowan *Kidsilk Aura* (75% kid mohair; 25% silk)
1 x ¾oz/25g skein (approx. 82yd/75m) each in:

A – Vintage 757
C – Raspberry 756
D – Wheat 752
E – Mallard 769
F – Damson 762
G – Forest 761
H – Terracotta 772
J – Pumice 768
K – Quarry Tile 760   R – Coral 774
L – Walnut 764   S – Loganberry 763
N – Cypress 755   2 x ¾oz/25g skeins each in:
Q – Sapphire 775   B – Orchard 771
P – Powder 753   M – Nearly Black 765

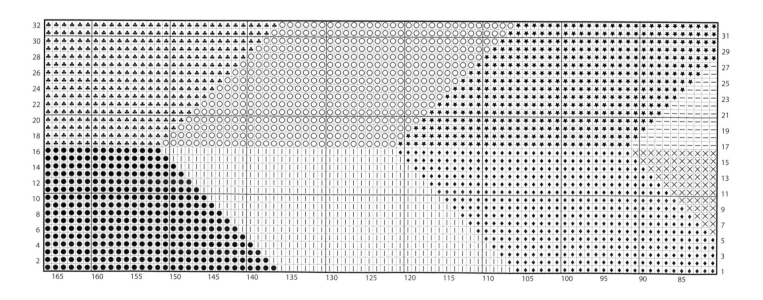

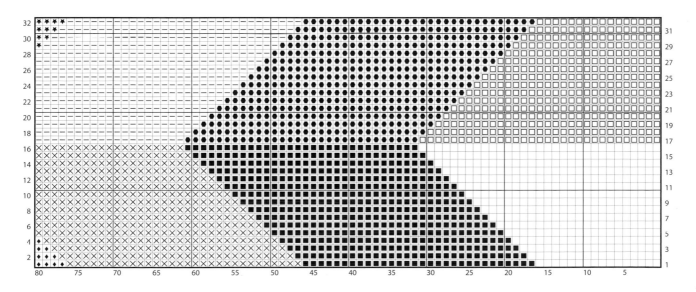

NEEDLES

1 pair size 10½ (7mm) knitting needles
1 pair size 10 (6mm) knitting needles
1 size 10 (6mm) circular knitting needle

GAUGE

14 sts and 18 rows = 4"/10cm measured over St st using size 10½ (7mm) needles *or size to obtain correct gauge.*

THROW

Using size 10½ (7mm) needles and A, cast on 166 sts.
Beg with a K row, working in St st throughout, using the intarsia technique and working the 32-row patt rep from chart on pages 124–125, cont until 288 rows and color layout diagram layout have been completed, ending with RS facing for next row.
Bind off.

CAST-ON/BOUND-OFF SIDE EDGINGS (both alike)

Using size 10 (6mm) needles and M, pick up and knit 166 sts evenly along cast-on/bound-off edge.
Working in garter st, inc 1 st at each end of 2nd and 5 foll alt rows. *178 sts.*
Knit 1 row.
Next row Using E, knit to end AND AT SAME TIME inc 1 st at each end of row. *180 sts.*
Bind off knitwise on WS.

SIDE EDGINGS (both alike)

Using size 10 (6mm) needles and M, pick up and knit 256 sts evenly along side edge.
Working in garter st rows, inc 1 st at each end of 2nd and 5 foll alt rows. *268 sts.*
Knit 1 row.
Next row Using E, knit to end AND AT SAME TIME inc 1 st at each end of row. *270 sts.*
Bind off knitwise on WS.

FINISHING

Press as described on the ball band.
Join sides of edges.

COLOR LAYOUT DIAGRAM

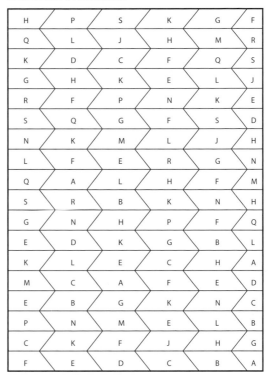

trapezoid cushion

Using a mercerized cotton yarn like Rowan *Cotton Glace* brings a brighter, fresher vibe to the basic trapezoid design, creating a very summery look. It is less forgiving when working in intarsia (see page 172), so take particular care when joining the yarns.

SKILL LEVEL ■■■□

FINISHED SIZE
18 x 15¾"/46 x 40cm

YARN
1 x 1¾oz/50g skein (approx. 126yd/115m) each of Rowan *Cotton Glace* (100% cotton)  in:
A – Bubbles 724
B – Dijon 739
C – Garnet 841
D – Ochre 833
E – Umber 838
F – Baked Red 837
G – Sky 749
H – Blood Orange 445
J – Persimmon 832
K – Twilight 829
L – Ivy 812
M – Candy Floss 747

NEEDLES AND EXTRAS
1 pair size 3 (3.25mm) knitting needles
1 piece of fabric, size to match cushion plus ¾"/2cm seam allowance on all sides

GAUGE
23 sts and 32 rows = 4"/10cm measured over St st using size 3 (3.25mm) needles *or size to obtain correct gauge.*

PATTERN NOTE
Work using the intarsia technique (see page 172).

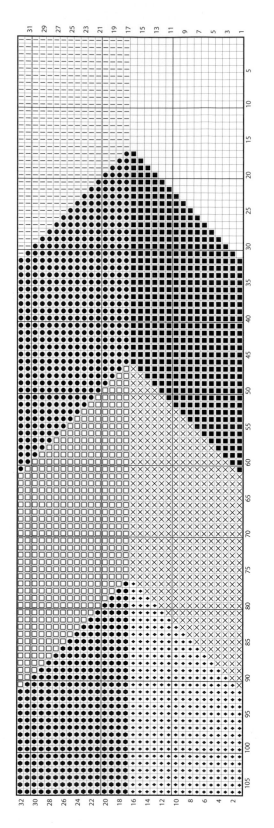

FRONT

Using A, cast on 106 sts.

Beg with a K row, working in St st throughout, using the intarsia technique and working the 32-row patt rep throughout, cont without shaping until 128 rows and color diagram layout have been completed, ending with RS facing for next row.

Bind off.

FINISHING

Press as described on the ball band.

Press seams. With RS facing, sew together the fabric back and knitted front with cushion form or stuffing inside.

KEY

☐ Color 1: Knit on RS, Purl on WS
■ Color 2: Knit on RS, Purl on WS
✕ Color 3: Knit on RS, Purl on WS
◆ Color 4: Knit on RS, Purl on WS
▯ Color 5: Knit on RS, Purl on WS
● Color 6: Knit on RS, Purl on WS
▢ Color 7: Knit on RS, Purl on WS
⬤ Color 8: Knit on RS, Purl on WS

COLOR LAYOUT DIAGRAM

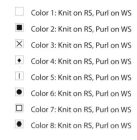

hyacinth scarf

This would be a brilliant beginner's project: the result has lots of color variety while still being simple to knit, thanks to the use of a shaded yarn like Regia *Design Line* random stripe. Mixing it in with a finer yarn like Rowan *Kidsilk Haze* gives it a great lift.

FINISHED SIZE
4¾ x 62"/12 x 157cm

YARN
1 x 3½oz/100g skein (approx. 450yd/420m) of Regia *Design Line* random stripe (75% wool; 25% polyamide) ❶ in Delphinium 2904
1 x ¾oz/25g skein (approx. 229yd/210m) of Rowan *Kidsilk Haze* (70% super kid mohair; 30% silk) ❸ in Smoke 831

NEEDLES
1 pair size 6 (4mm) knitting needles

GAUGE
21 sts and 35 rows = 4"/10cm measured over garter st using size 6 (4mm) needles *or size to obtain correct gauge.*

SCARF
Using both yarns held TOGETHER, cast on 1 st.
Row 1 (RS) (K1, yo, k1) into st. *3 sts.*
Row 2 and every foll alt row Knit.
Row 3 Inc in 1st 2 sts, k1. *5 sts.*
Row 5 Inc in 1st st, k2, inc in next st, k1. *7 sts.*
Row 7 Inc in 1st st, k4, inc in next st, k1. *9 sts.*
Cont to inc in this way until there are 33 sts, ending with RS facing for next row.
Next row K2tog, K to last 2 sts, inc in next st, k1.
Next row Knit.
Rep these 2 rows until scarf measures approx. 62"/157cm along side edge, ending with RS facing for next row.
Dec 1 st at each end of next and every foll alt row to 3 sts.
Work 1 row.
Next row K3tog. Fasten off.

rich shades

Whenever I'm designing colorways for my print collections
or knit designers, I always love the dark colorways best.
There is an intensity about deep colors that is so emotional
for me. Pools of dark purples, blues, and maroons can make
the hair stand up on the back of my neck. I particularly
loved designing the brilliant depths of the *Colourscape* yarns,
and the scarves in these tones look electric on a garment.
The bold geometry of the wiggle leg warmers and red circle
stole benefit from the darker palette. How different the half-
circle pattern appears in dark colors than the hot pastels on
page 58. I find deeper tones very flattering to wear, and I
hope you enjoy playing with these rich shades yourself.

red circle stole

These bold circles were inspired by the great Ballets Russes costume designer, Léon Bakst. He often used large-scale prints for theatrical effect. Huge circles were used more than once and caught my searching eye. I've done a leg of mutton jacket in these large circles. They seemed the perfect motif for a book like this, after the angular geometry of most of the motifs in it. I like the idea of massive circles in deep blood reds. I've designed a sock yarn that very subtly changes tone, so it just adds depth to the color rather than taking it into another tone altogether. I find these blushes of tone more effective sometimes than multicolor yarns. So, taking two of these subtly changing sock yarns, the navy becomes a good dark ground for my crimson circles.

SEE PAGE 154 FOR PATTERN

LEFT, BELOW, AND OVERLEAF The drama of these bold circles will cut a dash with many different outfits. The shaded yarn creates subtle tones within the circles, giving the colors a particular vibrancy. The stole is gorgeous to wear and handsome thrown over a couch or chair back.

dark dot scarf

I adore this yarn—there are some great colors, and it is thick enough to let you get on with it at a pace.

The darkness of these tones are great to wear as a highlight on a black outfit or a deep rich accent on tweeds or gray palettes. Even people who have never ventured into Fair Isle knitting before can manage this basic dot design. It's a great way to break into the rich possibilities of color knitting. From looking at the soft version of this design on page 24, you can see how playful this concept can be. Make your own choices and have fun.

SEE PAGE 156 FOR PATTERN.

LEFT Brandon and me (I am wearing the dark dot scarf) with the colorscape scarves (see page 142) in the background.
RIGHT The plummy foliage of the aptly named smokebush really makes the deep tones of the scarf glow.

diagonal colorscape scarves

Of all the projects in this book, I guarantee this scarf will hook you. You will very likely want to try it in several if not all the colorways of the *Colourscape* yarn. As you knit, the colors keep you constantly guessing as to what the next blush of tone will add to the whole. It is the perfect on-the-road project: one ball of yarn in your bag and any train or bus journey becomes a pleasure; or sitting by the fire or TV of an evening creating your web of color—delicious. It also amuses all who see you knitting the scarf, so is a good conversation piece. I loved designing this yarn but could not believe how entertaining it was to actually knit.

SEE PAGE 158 FOR PATTERN.

LEFT, BELOW, AND OVERLEAF
Like a kid in a candy store, the myriad colors of this yarn never fail to delight me, like those of the mosaics they are photographed against. See how the colors change with the diagonal knitting.

accordion stole

My trapezoid blanket (see page 100) kickstarted Brandon's ideas for this design. As he says, "With its silk and mohair yarn and formal geometry, it resembled parquet flooring or a piece of marquetry. Recently Kaffe had designed a gorgeous yarn for Regia called *Hand-dye Effect,* as a sock yarn, which has a subtle blush of one color group. It is very effective used in the blocks of color for any fine knits. I fed two versions of it, one navy tones and one shades of dark red, into the trapezoid motif as a long scarf. Not only is it a smaller scale, but limiting the colors makes the repetitions of arrowhead shapes become accordion-like in appearance. This transformation of a shape is amazing, and should give you many ideas of how to transform any design here to suit your taste."

SEE PAGE 160 FOR PATTERN.

LEFT A detail of the Arts and Crafts fireplace.
RIGHT The simple formality of this design is brought to life by this yarn as it delicately shades each lozenge shape. The decoration on the Moorcroft pot against the door plays with the same design principle.

ridged scarf

What a smoldering design of Brandon's this is! Here is Brandon's take on it: "This idea of a reverse stockinette stitch in a more or less solid tone with multicolor between the raised rows, is one that can apply to many other color moods. I love this hot crimson story. The reverse stockinette stitch really emphasizes the color. The subtle fragments of close tone below those raised rows are created by another faster-changing sock yarn. I love the way the caterpillarlike structure closes up as you wear it with only glimpses of the other yarn between.

This idea can be done in so many other moods. I've designed a peat brown *Hand-dye Effect* yarn, like the crimson one here, that I used as the reverse stockinette stitch ridges on a man's crew neck. It worked a treat for a darker feel (see *Regia Journal 2011*). I could see this idea being very dramatic with black ridges and smoldering deep tones of bottle green, maroon, peat, navy, and moss green between the rows.

For a larger version, perhaps a large stole, take two of Kaffe's *Colourscape* yarns in chunky and knit in the same fashion with one of them in reverse stockinette stitch ridges.

SEE PAGE 162 FOR PATTERN.

OPPOSITE The hot crimson and the raised design really stand out against this old oak church door.
BELOW LEFT Brandon in his velvet hat.
BELOW CENTER The crimson ridges show off the jewel-like shots of colorful stripes.
BELOW RIGHT A corner in my painting studio.

half-circle scarf

After the luscious pastel throw in half-circles on page 58, it was interesting to take the same graph to produce this dark, rich color mood. The wines and moss greens work so well worn with medium blue or navy, or even with a simple black outfit.

The *Pure Wool* range has many different colors, so you could really ring the changes on this layout. Try all reds, pinks, and oranges or blues, blacks, and purple. Very high contrast is good, too, really showing the graphic design. Navy, yellow, maroon, cream, and orange could be great, or blues and whites for a classic cool look. This pattern would also be interesting on a tiny scale. Very fine yarn and tiny needles would produce a tight, graphic look.

SEE PAGE 164 FOR PATTERN.

LEFT AND RIGHT It is interesting to see how this darker palette brings the background more to the fore. It has all the intensity of the stained-glass window (right).

wiggle scarf and leg warmers

There is something soothing yet lively about a meandering wavy line. I was fascinated by it first as a mosaic walkway. Here, I've knitted it in warm, deep colors with just enough contrast to define the exciting repeated graphic. I could definitely see this in a larger scale, using thicker yarns and needles to produce a big stole or bedspread. It would make a good sweater or jacket pattern, as well. Try it in any colors you fancy—high contrast would make it extra exciting, like the leg warmers seen here.

When we went to place these leg warmers in navy and magenta on our model, Candace Bahouth, whose house we were using, produced a great pair of black and magenta striped socks to match.

Imagine doing these in highest contrast, black and white—how sharp! You might wear them with two-toned black and white shoes. Shades of gray would look like the pebble mosaic walkway I first saw, and would be good with grays.

SEE PAGES 166 AND 168 FOR PATTERNS.

RIGHT Our model in the dramatic wiggle scarf and leg warmers, the warm terracotta tones echoing the lichens on this old church.
OPPOSITE The leg warmers with fun matching socks.

red circle stole

You will find that the Regia *Design Line Hand-dye Effect* yarn gives this piece great luster and strength. It makes a wonderfully firm knit, too, with a smooth, silky texture. Simple yet very effective.

SKILL LEVEL ■■■■

FINISHED SIZE
20½ x 92"/52 x 234cm

YARN
3 x 3½oz/100g skeins (each approx. 460yd/420m) of Regia *Design Line Hand-dye Effect* (75% merino wool; 25% nylon) ① in A – Regal 8857
2 x 3½oz/100g skeins (each approx. 460yd/420m) of Regia *Design Line Hand-dye Effect* (75% merino wool; 25% nylon) ① in B – Fuschia 8852

NEEDLES
1 pair size 5 (3.75mm) knitting needles
1 size 3 (3.25mm) circular knitting needle

GAUGE
23 sts and 33 rows to 4"/10cm measured over St st using size 5 (3.75mm) needles *or size to obtain correct gauge.*

PATTERN NOTE
Work using the intarsia technique (see page 172).

STOLE
Using size 5 (3.75mm) needles and A, cast on 110 sts.
Beg with a K row, work the 98 row patt rep from the chart throughout. Cont until work measures approx. 90¾"/230cm, ending with row 98 of patt and RS facing for next row.
Bind off.

EDGINGS
With RS facing, using size 3 (3.25mm) circular needle and A, pick up and knit 140 sts along cast-on/bound-off edges.
Beg with a P row and working in St st, cont as foll:
Inc 1 st at each end of 2nd and 3 foll alt rows. *148 sts.*
Next row (WS) Knit (to form ridge).

KEY

- ■ Yarn A: Knit on RS, Purl on WS
- ▨ Yarn B: Knit on RS, Purl on WS

Dec 1 st at each end of next and 3 foll alt rows. *140 sts.*
Work 1 row, ending with RS facing for next row.
Bind off.
With RS facing, using size 3 (3.25mm) circular needle, pick up and knit 644 sts along side edges.
Beg with a P row and working in St st cont as foll:

Inc 1 st at each end of 2nd and 3 foll alt rows. *652 sts.*
Next row (WS) Knit (to form ridge).
Dec 1 st at each end of next and 3 foll alt rows. *644 sts.*
Work 1 row, ending with RS facing for next row.
Bind off.

FINISHING

Press as described on the ball band.
Fold edges back at ridge line, join seams at corners, and sew borders loosely in position.

dark dot scarf

This makes a really good introduction to the Fair Isle technique (see page 170) for those who are new to working in color. I can't think of a better project to start on, because it has a really sophisticated result. The yarn knits up quickly, too.

SKILL LEVEL ◖■□□

FINISHED SIZE
12 x 67"/30 x 170cm

YARN
Rowan *Kidsilk Aura* (75% kid mohair; 25% silk) 🔳
1 x ¾oz/25g skein (approx. 82yd/75m) each in:
B – Nearly Black 765
C – Sapphire 775
D – Loganberry 763
E – Mallard 769
F – Walnut 764
G – Orchard 771
H – Damson 762
J – Raspberry 756
K – Cypress 755
2 x ¾oz/25g skeins (each approx. 82yd/75m) in:
A – Forest 761

NEEDLES
1 pair size 10½ (7mm) knitting needles

GAUGE
14 sts and 18 rows = 4"/10cm measured over St st using size 10½ (7mm) needles or *size to obtain correct gauge.*

SCARF
Using A, cast on 40 sts.
Knit 2 rows.
Beg with a K row and working in St st throughout, cont as foll:
Rows 1 to 4 Using A.
Row 5 * K2B, K2C, rep from * to end.
Rows 6 to 9 Using D.
Row 10 * K2C, K2B, rep from * to end.
Rows 11 to 14 Using A.
Row 15 As row 5.
Rows 16 to 19 Using E.
Row 20 As row 10.
Rows 21 to 24 Using A.
Row 25 As row 5.
Rows 26 to 29 Using F.
Row 30 As row 10.
Rows 31 to 34 Using A.
Row 35 As row 5.
Rows 36 to 39 Using G.
Row 40 As row 10.
Rows 41 to 44 Using A.
Row 45 As row 5.
Rows 46 to 49 Using H.
Row 50 As row 10.
Rows 51 to 54 Using A.
Row 55 As row 5.
Rows 56 to 59 Using J.
Row 60 As row 10.
Rows 61 to 64 Using A.
Row 65 As row 5.
Rows 66 to 69 Using K for version A and K for version B.
Row 70 As row 10.
These 70 rows set patt.
Cont in patt as set until work measures approx. 67"/170cm, ending with 4 rows of A, ending with facing for next row.
Knit 3 rows.
Bind off knitwise on WS.

diagonal colorscape scarves

This scarf is also great for novice knitters and again produces an elegant result with very few knitting skills needed, thanks to the exciting color qualities of the yarn, which is quick to knit with, too.

SKILL LEVEL

FINISHED SIZE
4¼ x 62¼" /11 x 158cm

YARN
1 x 3½oz/100g skein (approx. 175yd/160m) of Rowan *Colourscape Chunky* (100% lambswool) (5) shown here in Cherry 431, Carnival 430, Moody Blues 444, and Jungle 447

NEEDLES
1 pair size 10 (6mm) knitting needles

GAUGE
13.5 sts and 27 rows = 4"/10cm measured over garter st using size 10 (6mm) needles *or size to obtain correct gauge.*

SCARF
Cast on 1 st.
Row 1 (RS) (K1, yo, k1) into st. *3 sts.*
Row 2 and every foll alt row Knit.
Row 3 Inc in 1st 2 sts, k1. *5 sts.*
Row 5 Inc in 1st st, k2, inc in next st, k1. *7 sts.*
Row 7 Inc in 1st st, k4, inc in next st, k1. *9 sts.*
Cont to inc in this way until there are 21 sts, ending with RS facing for next row.
Next row K2tog, K to last 2 sts, inc in next st, k1.
Next row Knit.
Rep these 2 rows until scarf measures approx. 62¼"/158cm along side edge, ending with RS facing for next row.
Dec 1 st at each end of next and every foll alt row to 3 sts.
Work 1 row.
Next row K3tog. Bind off.

accordion stole

This is a grown-up project with a really strong graphic structure to it. It showcases the Regia *Design Line Hand-dye Effect* yarn, and its texture is perfect for this kind of throw, too, being firm and smooth.

SKILL LEVEL ■■■□

FINISHED SIZE
17½ x 53½"/44 x 136cm

YARN
1 x 3½oz/50g skein (approx. 460yd/420m) each of Regia *Design Line Hand-dye Effect* (70% wool; 25% polyamid; 5% acrylic) (1) in:
A – Night Tones 8855
B – Earthy 8856
C – Fuchsia 8852
D – Rhubarb 8854

NEEDLES
1 pair size 2 (2.75mm) knitting needles
1 size 2 (2.75mm) circular knitting needle

GAUGE
33 sts and 44 rows = 4"/10cm measured over St st using size 2 (2.75mm) needles *or size to obtain correct gauge.*

STOLE
Using A, cast on 134 sts.
Beg with a K row, work 5 rows in St st, ending with WS facing for next row.
Next row Knit (to form ridge).
Beg with a K row, working in St st throughout, beg and ending

rows as shown on chart A and working center 10 st rep 13 times, cont until all 6 rows have been worked.
Beg and ending rows as shown on chart A and working the center 40 st rep 3 times, working 30 row rep throughout, cont until work measures approx. 53¼"/135cm, ending after row 14 of pattern and RS facing for next row.
Beg and ending rows as shown on chart B and working 10 st rep 13 times, cont until all 6 rows have been worked.
Cont in A only.
Next row (RS) Purl (to form ridge).
Work 5 rows in St st.
Bind off.

FINISHING
Fold back cast-on/bound-off edge at ridge row and sew in place.

SIDE EDGINGS (both alike)
With RS facing, using size 2 (2.75mm) circular needle and A, pick up and knit 514 sts along side edge.
Beg with a P row and working in St st throughout, beg and ending rows as shown on chart A, cont until all 6 rows have been worked, ending with WS facing for next row.
Next row Knit (to form ridge).
Work 5 rows in St st.
Bind off.
Fold back side edging at fold line and sew in position.
Press as described on the ball band.

CHART A

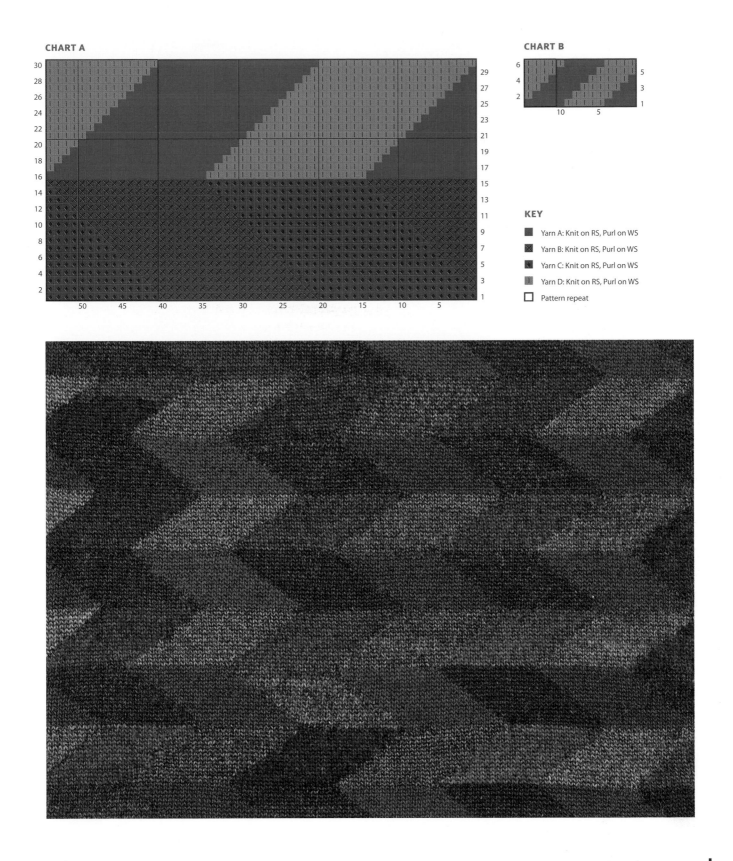

CHART B

KEY

- ■ Yarn A: Knit on RS, Purl on WS
- ▨ Yarn B: Knit on RS, Purl on WS
- ▧ Yarn C: Knit on RS, Purl on WS
- ▐ Yarn D: Knit on RS, Purl on WS
- ☐ Pattern repeat

ridged scarf

Another relatively simple project with great texture. These multicolored yarns really pull it off for this kind of scarf. Try making more than one in different colorways.

SKILL LEVEL ◼☐☐☐

FINISHED SIZE
8¼ x 56"/21 x 142cm

YARN
1 x 3½oz/100g skein (approx. 460yd/420m) of Regia *Hand-dye Effect* (70% wool; 25% polyamid; 5% acrylic) 🎱 in
A – Rubin 6550
1 x 3½oz/100g skein (approx. 460yd/420m) of Regia *Design Line Hand-dye Effect* (70% wool; 25% polyamid; 5% acrylic) 🎱 in B – Moor 2905

NEEDLES
1 pair size 3 (3.25mm) knitting needles

GAUGE
28 sts and 34 rows = 4"/10cm measured over St st using size 3 (3.25mm) needles *or size to obtain correct gauge.*

SCARF
Using A, cast on 59 sts.
Row 1 (RS) Using A, purl.
Row 2 Using A, knit.
Rows 3 and 4 As rows 1 and 2.
Row 5 Using B, knit.
Row 6 Using B, purl.
Rows 7 and 8 As rows 5 and 6.
These 8 rows set patt.
Cont in patt until scarf measures approx. 56"/142cm, ending with row 3 and WS facing for next row.
Bind off knitwise.

half-circle scarf

The myriad colors in the Rowan *Pure Wool 4 ply* make picking exciting color combinations really simple. If you don't want the edges to roll, you could turn them back or stitch the scarf to a backing fabric in earthy stripes.

SKILL LEVEL

FINISHED SIZE

13¾ x 49½"/35 x 125cm

YARN

Rowan *Pure Wool 4 ply* (100% superwash wool) **1**
2 x 1¾oz/50g skeins (each approx. 175yd/160m) in:
A – Port 437
1 x 1¾oz/50g skein (approx. 175yd/160m) each in:
B – Blue Iris 455
C – Quarry Tile 457
D – Havanna 458
E – Mocha 417
F – Hyacinth 426
G – Shale 402
H – Framboise 456
J – Glade 421

NEEDLES

1 size 3 (3.25mm) circular knitting needle

GAUGE

26 sts and 34 rows = 4"/10cm measured over St st using size 3 (3.25mm) circular needle *or size to obtain correct gauge.*

SCARF

Using A, cast on 325 sts.
Working back and forth cont as foll:
Knit 4 rows.
Beg with a K row, working in St st throughout, beg and ending rows as shown and working center 30 st rep 10 times, work 28 row rep throughout in colorways as shown on diagram.
Cont as set until all 112 rows have been worked, ending with RS facing for next row.
Using A, knit 3 rows.
Bind off knitwise on WS.

FINISHING

You may wish to turn back and sew a seam to stop the edges from rolling.

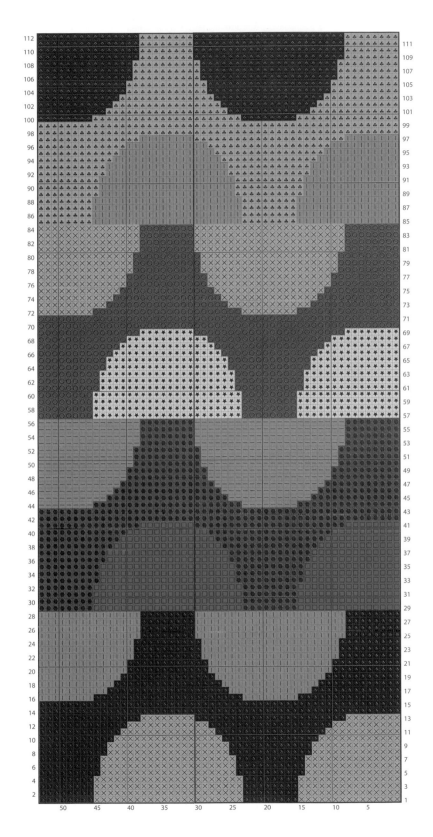

wiggle leg warmers

This legwear cannot fail to get you noticed! You work this one in rounds with a relatively simple repeat.

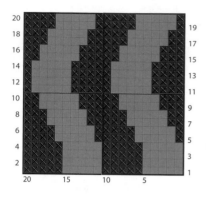

SKILL LEVEL

FINISHED SIZE
17 x 12¼"/43 x 31cm

YARN
1 x 1¾oz/50g skein (approx. 175yd/160m) each of Rowan *Pure Wool 4 ply* (100% superwash wool) **1** in A – Hyacinth 426
1 x 1¾oz/50g skein (approx. 175yd/160m) each of Rowan *Cashsoft 4 ply* (57% extrafine merino wool; 33% acrylic microfiber; 10% cashmere) **1** in B – Deep 431

NEEDLES
1 size 3 (3.25mm) circular knitting needle

GAUGE
28 sts and 36 rows = 4"/10cm measured over St st using size 3 (3.25mm) circular needle *or size to obtain correct gauge.*

LEG WARMERS (make 2)
Using A, cast on 120 sts.
Work in rounds not rows and ensure sts are not twisted when joining.
Round 1 * K2, p2, rep from * to end.
This round sets rib.
Work 11 rounds more in rib.
Working 10 sts as set on chart 12 times in each round, cont as set on chart, working rows 1 to 20 throughout until work measures 10½"/27cm.
Using A, work 12 rows in rib.
Bind off in rib. Press as described on the ball band.

KEY
■ Yarn A: Knit on RS, Purl on WS
▨ Yarn B: Knit on RS, Purl on WS
□ Pattern repeat

useful information

COLOR KNITTING TECHNIQUES

This book is all about knitting in color. When you are knitting in more than one color the method you choose will be determined by how the colors are used in the pattern. The knitting method you choose when knitting with more than one color is governed by how the colors are used in the pattern. Where a pattern calls for two colors to be changed every few stitches in a row, the best method to use is one called **Fair Isle**, in which the non-working color yarn is stranded (ie carried behind the work) when not being knitted. There are two ways to work this: one is the usual knitting technique (one-handed) and the other is to use one hand to manipulate the non-working yarn while the other does the actual knitting (two-handed).

Larger blocks of color are tackled using the **intarsia** technique (see page 172), since you do not want to have long strands of yarn across the back of the work

(although you can catch the yarn at the back of the work using techniques known as weaving or twisting). In the intarsia technique you work with the blocks of colors on separate balls or bobbins. To prevent holes forming in the work, or cutting off and weaving in lots of loose ends, you normally twist the new yarn in with the working yarn when it is introduced. The method varies according to whether the color change is vertical or on a diagonal slant.

When working in intarsia and changing colors in a vertical line, the yarns must be twisted on every row. When changing colors on a diagonal line, the yarns must only be twisted on every other row. If the diagonal slants to the right, twist the yarns only on knit rows. If the diagonal slants to the left, twist the yarns only on purl rows.

Fair Isle knitting

STRANDING—ONE-HANDED

1 On the knit side, drop the working yarn. Bring the new color (now the working yarn) over the top of the dropped yarn and work to the next color change.

2 Drop the working yarn. Bring the new color under the dropped yarn and work to the next color change. Repeat steps 1 and 2.

1 On the purl side, drop the working yarn. Bring the new color (now the working yarn) over the top of the dropped yarn and work to the next color change.

2 Drop the working yarn. Bring the new color under the dropped yarn and work to the next color change. Repeat steps 1 and 2.